D0428092

RESHAPING

How to Turn Dissatisfaction into Contentment

A JEALOUS HEART

A l i c e F r y l i n g

INTERVARSITY PRESS
DOWNERS GROVE, ILLINOIS 60515

To Bob—I love you.

InterVarsity Press® is the book-publishing division of InterVarsity Christian Fellowship®, a student movement active on campus at hundreds of universities, colleges and schools of nursing in the United States of America, and a member movement of the International Fellowship of Evangelical Students. For information about local and regional activities, write Public Relations Dept., InterVarsity Christian Fellowship, 6400 Schroeder Rd., P.O. Box 7895, Madison, WI 53707-7895.

ISBN 0-8308-1629-1

Printed in the United States of America ∞

Library of Congress Cataloging-in-Publication Data

Fryling, Alice.
    Reshaping a jealous heart: how to turn dissatisfaction into contentment/Alice Fryling; foreword by Karen Mains.
        p.   cm.
    Includes bibliographical references.
    ISBN 0-8308-1629-1
    1. Jealousy—Religious aspects—Christianity.   I. Title.
BV4627.J43F79   1993
241'.3—dc20

93-42725
CIP

15 14 13 12 11 10 9 8 7 6 5 4 3 2 1
04 03 02 01 00 99 98 97 96 95 94

Foreword

William Shakespeare comments on the sin of envy in several of his plays. In Henry VIII, the character Wolsey laments, "Of what coarse metal ye are moulded, envy: / How eagerly ye follow my disgraces / As if it fed ye! and how sleek and wanton / Ye appear in every thing may bring my ruin!"

Several years ago, I became suddenly aware that I was guilty of the sin of envy. What a surprise! I had always equated envy with the green-eyed monster named jealousy, and I knew I was not a jealous person. Jealousy shouted. But envy? For me, envy was more subtle, quiet and devious—curling, at my discovery, near the bottom of my soul.

As it turned out, at root the two are not very different at all.

One Bible encyclopedia defines envy as "a grudging regard for the advantages seen to be enjoyed by others." What did I envy? I discovered a grudging regard for the advantages seen to be enjoyed by others. I envied those people who didn't have to juggle ten balls in the air at the same time. They only had four balls to juggle, and they tossed them so proficiently. I tossed a mother ball, a broadcaster ball, a wife ball, a housewife ball, a writer ball, a be-a-friend ball, a church member ball— and frankly, I was not so proficient as those I envied. I kept dropping two or three of my bouncing balls.

I found that envy in me was an insidious sin—because it was so quiet—and that it separated me from the very people I needed to know. I held a grudging regard for those enjoying advantages which I wanted but did not have. I withdrew. I cooled in their company. I withheld myself. But I've discovered an antidote for my sin of envy. After confession, after repentance, after seeking a change of heart, I swallow a dose of this quick cure. The remedy is intentionality. The moment I find grudging regard gnawing quietly, I sit myself down and intentionally celebrate the people involved. I concentrate on the beauty of their uniqueness. In my heart, I deliberately applaud their accomplishments. I may even send them a note saying, "Well done!"

And instead of allowing the enemy of my soul to isolate me with his separate-and-destroy tactics, I feel warmth; love binds me to the ones I have envied. Instead of begrudging them their successes, I begin to learn from these others who have so much to teach me about focused living.

After looking at envy in my own soul, I have become convinced that it is envy in the church—envy and jealousy—that prohibits much of God's work in and through us. As Exeter, another Shakespearean character, says, "When envy breeds unkind division / There comes the ruin, there begins confusion."

If you are discovering jealousy or envy lurking in yourself, I would strongly recommend another act of intentionality: read and study this book. Commune with it privately or with a group of friends or in a Sunday-school class. This thoughtful presentation has the potential to disgorge the underground currents, those subtexts of emotion that are breeding "unkind division."

Take the remedy. Be intentional. Examine envy and jealousy. In humility, read these pages. You, like Alice Fryling and me, may discover some surprising truths about yourself.

Karen Mains

Preface

This is a book about jealousy. But even more, it is a book about relationships. Our relationships with family and friends—and with God.

What makes relationships work? Or *not* work? Why are some satisfying and others empty? What about my relationship with God? What makes it full of joy and peace? And what makes me sometimes squirm and fret under his watchful eye? I have an endless supply of questions like these! You may have them too.

Usually my questions bring me pleasure. But sometimes they challenge me and hurt me. One of the days when my questions hurt was the day we went to the Minneapolis Zoo.

We were there with friends, four parents and four children. It was Teddy Bear Day at the zoo, and if we had each brought a teddy bear, we could have gotten in free. But we didn't know that, and our bears were all home in bed, so we paid for our tickets and trooped into the park.

We laughed at the dolphins and admired the penguins. We looked up at the giraffes, and they looked down at us. We watched mother ducks lead their young babies around in the water. Then we went to the lions. Standing in front of the lion exhibit, I began to cry. Tears streamed down my face. My family and friends were astonished. What was wrong? Was I sad because we didn't have our teddy bears and had to pay for our tickets? No, of course not. Or had they offended me without knowing it? No, not at all. Why, then, was I crying?

I wasn't really sure myself. But I knew more about what was going on inside me than they did. I knew that when I woke up that morning I had felt very sad. I knew that I was disappointed in myself and in several other people. I knew that my relationships with those I loved were not what they should be. Why couldn't I love them as I wanted to, and why did I fear that they did not love me?

Standing in front of the lion exhibit, I saw several regal lions wandering around among rocks and bushes. They were gorgeous creatures. But I knew that if I were unprotected by the zoo's fences, I would need to be afraid of those lions. They were dangerous. As I thought about facing them alone, I felt deep fear.

I remembered the Bible's statement (I thought) that someday the lion will lie down with the lamb. Did that mean that someday a small, unprotected lamb will be able to curl up and sleep within the embrace of a powerful lion? Later I found out that what the Bible actually promises is that the lamb will be able to live with the wolf, and that a calf will be able to live together with a lion (Is 11:6). But that day at the zoo, I was right about God's promise: Someday there will be peace, both in the animal kingdom and in the human kingdom. Someday my life will be at peace, and my relationships will be filled with love rather than anxiety, with kindness rather than envy, with patience rather than pressure. As I thought about what that would be like, I began to cry. I cried for all that was wrong with the world *now*. I cried for all the pain in my life that day. I cried because I didn't know if I could wait until the time when, by God's grace, the lion and the lamb would lie down together. How was I to live my life in the meantime? Where could I find peace and love on this side of God's promised redemption?

I honestly don't remember the rest of the day at the zoo. I

assume I dried my tears and told my friends not to worry. We probably visited the elephants and the camels, I don't know. But I do remember the questions I wrestled with. In some ways, without the tears and the lions, I ask those questions every day. I care very deeply about my relationships with others and with God. I want to live in love and peace. But I don't always know how. That's why I decided to do some study—and then to write this book.

Our relationships with others, this side of heaven, are not always peaceful. They are sometimes far from loving. The lion is not yet lying down with the lamb. I am not yet able to give or to receive love perfectly, as I will be when "perfection comes" (1 Cor 13:10). My life is still ravaged by the effects of sin, my own sin and the sin of others.

The sins which destroy relationships come under many guises. Pride hurts relationships. Insecurity handicaps our ability to love. Unbridled hostility thwarts our attempts to experience intimacy. Jealousy destroys our efforts to love and to encourage those close to us.

As we look for answers to our questions about relationships, we could look at any one of these effects of sin. I have chosen to look specifically at jealousy because we do not talk about it very much, and yet it permeates many of our friendships, thwarting them and frustrating us in our attempts to love others. Jealousy can attack a relationship and do painful damage before we even know it is lurking nearby. At the zoo, animals and people alike are protected from danger. But our lives are seldom neatly fenced to protect our friendships and relationships. The enemy can attack before we know what is happening. And jealousy is one of his favorite weapons!

In this book we will confront the dangerous, insidious power of jealousy. We'll look at ways we can limit its destruction this

side of heaven. And we'll consider ways we can learn to obey
God and experience more of his love in our lives.

I want these chapters to be very real and very personal. And
very biblical. We can conquer sin and temptation in our lives
only when we are honest enough to admit it and concerned
enough to work at applying specific biblical truth to specific
situations in our daily lives. This is a very personal experience,
even when it happens in the context of fellowship with our
friends. To help you apply what you are learning to the needs
of your own heart, I have included questions at the end of each
chapter for use in your own devotions or as part of a small
group. These questions are different from typical Bible study
questions: my intent is to help you meditate rather than
analyze, apply rather than theorize. Use them in the way that
works best for you. I hope the verses I have chosen will help
you pray. I hope they will help you look at your own life in light
of biblical truth. And I hope they will help you take steps toward
growth and obedience.

Some of what I write I have learned directly from these
Scriptures. Some things I have learned from painful mistakes.
Some things I am just now learning. But of one thing I am
sure—God loves us and he wants us to be able to love one
another. Someday all our relationships will be entirely loving.

I believe God is pleased when we take steps to learn anything
we can do now to grow in our capacity to love. Then, someday,
the lamb will be able to lie down with both the lion and the wolf.

1

Sometimes It's Hard to Love My Neighbor

*M*y tears that day at the zoo reflected big questions deep within my heart. I was asking what was wrong with my life. I was asking what was wrong with my world, how I could continue to live in such an imperfect environment. Looking back, I can see that, in my tears, I was crying out to God. The spirit he had placed within me was calling to him. In a confused, nonverbal way, I was saying to God, "Lord, I need you to put the pieces of my life together. I need you to touch my soul. I need you to give life and love to my closest relationships. Lord, I believe! Help my unbelief!"

It is comforting to know that I am not alone in my questions about life. Some people ask them with their minds. Some people ask them with their hearts. Some ask eagerly, wanting to know the answers right now. Some ask theoretically, even rhetorically. But one way or another, questions about life and relationships have been around since the beginning of time.

Philosophers, teachers and religious leaders have asked questions, and answered them, throughout the ages. Socrates, St. Augustine, Shakespeare, Lincoln. Many great thinkers have contributed to our understanding of ourselves and of human relationships.

But the person who intersected history most poignantly was Jesus of Nazareth. What he taught about life is more helpful to me than the wisdom of all the other philosophers combined. So I sit up and listen (when I am not crying in the zoo!) as I read Jesus' words. I note how he answers my questions. I identify with his hearers when I read about his interactions with his contemporaries. I am more than mildly interested in Jesus' answers to the questions asked by the religious leaders of his day.

One question stands out above the rest: "Of all the commandments," a Pharisee asked, "which is the most important?" (Mk 12:28). That's my question too. In twentieth-century terms, with its proliferation of knowledge, ever-increasing speed of communication, mind-boggling modern technology, what is the most important thing I can do with my life? My question is not primarily theological, or even theoretical, as the Pharisee's question may have been. But whatever his intent, I'm glad he asked. Because I too want to know, What is the most important commandment of all?

"The most important one," answered Jesus, "is this: 'Hear, O Israel, the Lord our God, the Lord is one. Love the Lord your God with all your heart and with all your soul and with all your mind and with all your strength.' The second is this: 'Love your neighbor as yourself.' There is no commandment greater than these" (Mk 12:29-31).

If I understand Jesus correctly, he is saying that the most important thing I can do in life is to love God and to love others.

All my activities, abilities and interests fall under the influence of the commandments *to love*. I am committed to that truth. I am committed to try to obey these two great commandments. So why is it so incredibly difficult to do that?

There are a lot of reasons why we struggle to love God and why we struggle to love each other. There were a lot of reasons why I cried at the zoo. But I believe that one of the primary reasons we struggle in our relationships is that *we live with distorted views of ourselves and of God.* Instead of believing truth, we believe lies. We believe we can control life. We think we are in charge. We believe that God is not involved in our lives, that he doesn't care and that we have to look out for ourselves.

I Deserve More!

Jealousy is one result of this kind of distorted thinking. Jealousy, by my definition, is *dissatisfaction with myself and my life because I believe I deserve more than I am getting.* When I look at life through jealous eyes, I see all the opportunities, rewards and creature comforts that others have, or that the world promises, and I say to myself and to God, "I want it. I want it all. I want it now."

Jealousy is one of the outcomes of the Fall of humanity from the arms of God. In the first three chapters of Genesis we see the record of Adam and Eve, to whom God had given many good gifts. But God did not give them everything. There was one tree, in the middle of the garden, that Adam and Eve could not have. Sin came into the world because this first man and woman ate fruit from a tree that God had not given to them. The result of that action was not an increased awareness of God but an increased awareness of themselves, their nakedness, their fears and their guilt.

Adam and Eve sacrificed perfection in their relationship with God and with each other *because they wanted it all.* That began a pattern for relationships that has continued throughout history. Jesus taught about how to mend those relationships. And in his death Jesus restored us to our loving Father, so we have the sure hope that someday love will reign again.

But in the meantime, we struggle with sin. We struggle to love God with all our hearts and souls and minds and strength. We struggle to love our neighbors as ourselves. We struggle, among other things, with jealousy.

Jealousy is why it was almost impossible for Jeff, the leader of his youth group, to love Paul when Paul arrived on the scene with twice as much up-front talent as Jeff would ever have.

Jealousy is why it was so hard for me to love my friend who bought a brand-new, state-of-the-art sewing machine while I was still saving my pennies to try to afford a used one.

Jealousy is one reason why it is sometimes hard to love the people in church who seem so sophisticated and "together."

Jealousy is why it was hard for Andy, Steve and Kate to love each other as they vied for the attention of the company president.

Jealousy is why it is hard for Skip, a realtor, to love his realtor friend who just sold a $500,000 home.

Jealousy is why Rick, a talented vocalist, struggled to love Jay when Jay won the state competition for collegiate musicians.

These are the kinds of struggles that wreak havoc in our lives and interfere with our intention to obey Jesus.

Jealousy is not the only thing that destroys relationships. And, in fact, everything we call jealousy is not really jealousy. What we call sin is not always sin. But it will serve us well to stop and take a long, hard look at jealousy. Underneath jealous feelings we will probably find fear, pride, anger, covetousness and ambition. It will not always be pleasant to be honest about our jealousy. I would rather talk about my loving, joyful inclinations. But when we get close to people, our relationships are affected by our negative emotions as well as by the positive ones. If I choose to feel only certain emotions, I risk becoming a person who is emotionally distant from others. Total emotional distance is a sickness.

One of the dangerous things that sometimes happens in relationships is comparison. When I look at my friends and acquaintances and compare myself with them, I usually come up short. I live in a relational world, and comparisons come with the territory. By watching other people, I learn, I grow, I experience new ways of relating. But when watching turns to comparing, I suffer. I am apt to compare my weaknesses with other people's strengths. First mistake. Then I search my mind for a few of my strengths to hold up to their weaknesses. Second mistake. Then I generalize their weaknesses to make them into major character flaws. In fact, I say to myself, *I don't think I like that person after all!* The stain of jealousy begins to seep into the way I relate to them.

I asked several friends to tell me how jealousy impacts their lives. Here are a few of their comments:

"Sometimes I think jealousy is not just wanting something, but wanting it exclusively—to be the only one, or one of the few, who has this experience, this relationship or this thing."

"There is a big temptation, especially in Christian circles, to be jealous of relationships. Sometimes this may be because of the prestige the relationship gives. But for me (an extrovert), it's the healing or energizing qualities a relationship may give—so I'm jealous if I don't have it."

"Jealousy doesn't sit very long with me—it quickly deteriorates into depression and feelings of personal failure."

"Jealousy, for me, is not only emotional and intellectual, but also somewhat physical—I feel tense, upset, angry. I may even cry."

"As a Christian, when I first experienced jealousy, it was closely followed by guilty feelings and shame, because 'Christians shouldn't be jealous'!"

"For me, when I am envious of someone's house or money, that jealousy spills over into our relationship. Because I don't like the envious, jealous feelings I have, I distance myself. Then not only do I have these feelings, but I miss the joy of the friendship."

"I get jealous when I see another Christian have something I think I deserve. I not only get mad at the person, but I get mad at God as well."

"It's when I am feeling fragile that I am most vulnerable to jealousy. Maybe I hope that something—money, prestige, a house—will help bandage the wound within."

These comments highlight something very basic: *Jealousy has as much to do with how I view myself as with how I view others.* This fits with Jesus' assumption that loving my neighbor has to do with my attitude toward myself. "Love your neighbor as yourself," he said. When I ask myself, "*Why* am I jealous?" I may need to take a hard look inside myself to find the answer.

Not an External Matter

Henri Nouwen writes about what might be going on inside ourselves when he describes the emotions of a "lost soul," one who has moved away from the love and acceptance of his heavenly Father:

It goes somewhat like this: I am not so sure anymore that I

have a safe home, and I observe other people who seem to be better off than I. I wonder how I can get to where they are. I try hard to please, to achieve success, to be recognized. When I fail, I feel jealous or resentful of these others. When I succeed, I worry that others will be jealous or resentful of me. I become suspicious or defensive and increasingly afraid that I won't be what I so much desire or will lose what I already have. Caught in this tangle of needs and wants, I no longer know my own motivations. I feel victimized by my surroundings and distrustful of what others are doing or saying. Always on my guard, I lose my inner freedom and start dividing the world into those who are for me and those who are against me. I wonder if anyone really cares. I start looking for validations of my distrust. And wherever I go, I see them, and I say: "No one can be trusted." And then I wonder whether *anyone* really loved me.[1]

So the answer to *why* I am jealous has to do with what goes on inside my heart. The answer to *how* I can overcome my jealousy has to do with understanding what goes on inside the heart of our loving heavenly Father. As we study jealousy together, we will find two focal points: "Who am I?" and "Who is God?"

My relationships with others clearly grow out of my relationship with God. When I understand how much God loves me, when I understand his kindness and graciousness to me, then I bow down in love and worship before him. And this act of worship changes my relationship with others, because it motivates me to choose to love my neighbor as myself.

Jealousy, obviously, interferes with my ability to make that choice. But we should not look at jealousy primarily as a sin to be confessed and forgotten. Rather, let's see jealousy as a rope. It is made up of many threads, wrapped around our necks, waiting to strangle us. We can take apart the rope and, by looking at each thread, break its ability to destroy our relationships with those we are trying to love. Some of the threads are emotional, some are theological, some are from our past, but they lose their power to injure us when they are not intertwined in the form of jealousy.

It is not easy to talk about jealousy. Actually, it is embarrassing. For many people it is easier to talk about sexual sins and other forms of immorality. For most, it is easier to be theoretical and to blame others rather than admit to jealous feelings. But until we acknowledge the reality of jealousy (we all experience it) and look at the ingredients that go into it (whether we like them or not), we will be victims of its devastation.

Let us look at jealousy, then, with the intent to find freedom. As we seek to untangle its deceitful threads, we will need to be honest about ourselves and work hard in our quest for truth. Truth sets us free. Truth comes from Jesus. Jesus taught us to love God and love one another. He will enable us to do that.

Scripture for Reflection or Discussion

1. "Hear, O Israel: The LORD our God, the LORD is one. Love the LORD your God with all your heart and with all your soul and with all your strength. These commandments that I give you today are to be upon your hearts. Impress them on your children. Talk about them when you sit at home and when you walk along the road, when you lie down and when you get up. Tie them as symbols on your hands and bind them on your foreheads. Write them on the doorframes of your houses and on your gates" (Deut 6:4-9).

Loving God and obeying his commandments go hand in hand. Think about your daily activities. What can you do to make sure you are loving God with your heart, your soul and your strength? What can you do that would be similar to the Israelites' writing verses on their doorframes and their gates?

2. "Each one should test his own actions. Then he can take pride in

himself, without comparing himself to somebody else" (Gal 6:4).
How and when do you "test your own actions"? In what areas of
your life do you think God wants you to take pride? In what areas
of your life are you most apt to compare yourself with others in an
unhealthy way?

3. "Are you not in error because you do not know the Scriptures or
the power of God?" (Mk 12:24).
These are the words Jesus spoke to the Sadducees when they
challenged Jesus with their questions. How do you think ignorance
of Scripture and lack of appreciation for the power of God limits us
in our struggle with sin, including jealousy?

2

There's Mildew
in My Soul!

*T*ears *squeezed out of my eyes*
(again!) as I drove home from Sheila's house. As I stopped at a
traffic light, I pounded on the steering wheel. "Lord, *why,* if you
are going to give me a mansion in heaven, can't I have a bigger
house right now?" I loved Sheila and counted her as a good
friend. But I had never seen her home—until today. Now I knew:
Sheila lived in the house of my dreams.

By the time I pulled into my own driveway, my emotions were
shot. I faced the rest of the day in a depressed and confused
state of discontent. I experienced, in living color, the truth of
Proverbs 14:30: "Envy rots the bones."

Rot is a good word for envy or jealousy. The decay caused by
rottenness can cause houses to collapse, it can spoil food, it
can cause life-threatening disease. But rot is often unseen at
first. Mildew seeps into the box of Christmas ornaments stored

in the basement. Mold takes over the loaf of bread we were saving for Saturday's lunch. Decay in our bodies is often ignored until pain compels us to respond.

The rot of envy is like that. We often do not notice the immediate effects of our jealous thoughts. Decay can creep into our faith, quietly and unheeded. We do not usually decide to "unbelieve" God. We just forget to believe. Or we believe untruth. Or we allow sin to take precedence over belief. One way or another, we silently give up a little of our faith. We don't *intend* to allow weakness and decay to invade our faith, but just as surely as mildew will invade that box of Christmas decorations, so deterioration will invade our spiritual lives if we give in to sins such as envy and jealousy.

Envy and jealousy become seeds of bitterness which take root in our hearts. The bitterness grows into a parasite, sustaining itself by feeding off the relationships which mean the most to us. The parasite wraps itself around our hearts and our minds. Eventually it creeps into our souls, touching even our relationship with God.

Envy and jealousy have slightly different dictionary meanings. Jealousy is "resentment against a rival or against another's success or advantage"; envy is "a feeling of discontent at seeing another's superiority, advantages or success."[1] But at the moment when the rot of envy and jealousy invades our hearts, the dictionary distinctions become theoretical. Whatever it is called, what hurts me is that I want something you have. Or I want to be who you are. Or I want to do what you do. If I cannot have what you have, be who you are or do what you do, then I don't want you to have any of these experiences or possessions either. Even if you are not really the person I think you are, even if what you have isn't actually all that great, jealousy and envy still make me suspicious that

I am missing out on something.

It is not that God does not want us to have "wish lists." On the contrary, our heavenly Father says he will give us the desires of our hearts (Ps 37:4). He compares himself to earthly fathers who love to give good gifts to their children (Mt 7:11). No, the issue with envy and jealousy is that we want what God has chosen to give to someone else.

Devastating and Destructive

Jealousy does more than rot the bones. It is more overwhelming than anger (Prov 27:4). Unseen and often unacknowledged, it can keep us stuck in life's ruts, hamper our growth and blind us to our weaknesses. Jealousy is a vicious circle. It is rooted in a false view of God, ourselves and others—and jealousy, in turn, further distorts our view of God and our opinion of ourselves.

Paul could not teach the Corinthians deep spiritual truths because of their quarreling and their jealousy. Jealousy made them remain spiritual infants, drinking spiritual milk rather than eating solid food (1 Cor 3:2). James says that coveting, or desiring things we cannot have, wreaks havoc in our relationships (Jas 4:1-2). The author of Ecclesiastes pessimistically observes that "all labor and all achievement spring from man's envy of his neighbor" (Eccles 4:4). Furthermore, he says, "Whoever loves money never has money enough; whoever loves wealth is never satisfied with his income" (Eccles 5:10). Whether our envy grows out of our desire for wealth, position or power, jealousy, like all other sin, is a dead-end street. Exposing the roots of our own jealous thoughts will free us to grow to become the people God created us to be.

Jealousy in my own life is a very, very silent sin. It is deeply rooted, but few people see it. Until recently I did not think of myself as a jealous person, because my kind of jealousy is not what most people think of at first. Yes, I wish I had Sheila's house, I wish I had Joan's body and Jim's talent. But those jealousies are like mild colds compared to the jealousies deep within. Each of us has a few areas which are particularly susceptible to the rot of jealousy. For some it may be in the area of romance. For others it may be in athletics. Others may have a passion for community recognition, good looks or academic achievement.

If the truth be told, the jealousies that trouble me most are those which seep into an area of my life which is very close to my heart: the area of ministry. To be able to serve God and to welcome people into his kingdom is one of my most important values. And it is there that the rot of jealousy often sets in.

A Very Persistent Sin

Looking back, I can see the danger of jealousy early in my Christian life, when I was in college. After I arrived on campus at the University of Maryland, I discovered that there were at least three evangelical Christian groups on campus, plus a variety of denominational and other religious groups. I looked around and decided that I fit best into the fellowship of InterVarsity. In my dorm I met Karen, an effervescent, bubbly Christian who had chosen Campus Crusade for Christ as her student group on campus. For the next nine months, I struggled with jealousy as Karen told me about her friends who were coming to Crusade meetings. Never mind that my friends were coming to InterVarsity meetings. I wanted them *all.* I wanted to be the best, the most effective witness in my dorm. What a shame! How sad God must have felt as he watched me struggle with jealousy. And how sad that my friendship with Karen was blocked by the rot of envy.

My hopes that struggles with jealousy would abate at graduation turned out to be ill-founded. After graduation I decided to continue working with InterVarsity as a staff member. As sad and ridiculous as it seems now, I transferred my jealousy of my fellow students to my fellow staff members.

I remember one evening in particular. Cindy and I were staffing a campus mission in Pennsylvania. We sat together in a local student hangout, eating hamburgers and sharing fries. Cindy told me with breathless excitement and a measure of exhaustion that she was overwhelmed with the number of students she was meeting at the mission. They all seemed to want to get together with her privately. She pulled out her overstuffed appointment book to see if she could fit one more hour into the next day.

I can tell you now that French fries and jealousy are not a good mix! The fries sat like lead in my stomach as jealousy gripped my heart. I didn't have an overstuffed appointment book. I could easily remember the few students who had asked to see me. How I wished I could be like Cindy, with a schedule too full to keep in her head! And, once again, how sad that must have made my Father in heaven.

Here's a bit of irony, though. Twenty years later I found out that at the very same time when I was jealous of Cindy, she was jealous of me! She thought I was so intelligent and wise! What a ridiculous state of affairs. If it weren't for the tremendous loss of human energy, it would be funny. But jealousy is rarely funny for long. When I think of the loss of creativity, fellowship and ministry opportunities that I experienced because of my jealousy, I can only weep. Love can "rejoice with those who rejoice" (Rom 12:15). Love would have rejoiced that so many students wanted to see Cindy. Love would have rejoiced at any amount of God-given wisdom someone had. But jealousy cannot rejoice. Jealousy is a tool of Satan. He uses it to weaken our resolve and destroy our attempts to minister in Jesus' name.

Don't Lose Hope

But the battle is not over. And I can think of three good reasons why we can have hope as we face Satan's assaults.

The first reason is that *the very tool which Satan uses to destroy, God may use to convict and bring growth.* St. Ambrose, fourth-century bishop of Milan, is said to have written: "The Devil tempts that he may ruin; God tests that he may crown."

Not long ago my husband, Bob, had surgery which required many internal and external stitches. Just as he regained his strength and reentered normal life, the area of the incision began to hurt. I immediately assumed the worst—a secondary infection which would send him back to the operating room. My relief was great when a nurse explained that the pain was caused by the growing back of nerve endings which had been cut in surgery.

Our jealousy may be like that. We don't like the pain it causes. It may even scare us. But, by God's grace, our jealousy may be like Bob's awakening nerves. If they had not grown back, he would not have been in pain at that time, but years from now he would have no nerve endings to warn him of danger. Some pain is good pain. Our jealousy may be that kind of pain—awakening nerves, an internal awareness which lets us know that something is wrong in our relationship with God and our relationships with others.

My jealousy of Karen and Cindy was painful, but eventually it helped me see that I was living under a false assumption. I thought I was serving God, but I was also serving my own ego, or my own need to be needed and to be loved. My jealousy, then, could have been a call to confession, a prompting to reorder my priorities, a reminder to renew my commitment to my Lord. I don't remember if those things actually occurred at that time, but growth was beginning. I'm thankful that God always welcomes beginnings. We may need to throw away the mildewed Christmas ornaments or the moldy bread, but it is never, ever too late for God to work in our lives. No matter what the struggle, God can take what Satan means for evil and bring it to good.

The second reason I can have hope in the midst of the battle with jealousy is that *human jealousy does not necessarily stop God from fulfilling his own goals*. In the Old Testament we read the story of a young man, Joseph, whose brothers were green with jealousy over Joseph's favored position in the family. Their jealousy led them to actually sell their brother as a slave, to be carried out of the country. Hundreds of years later, Stephen, one of the first martyrs of the early church, had this to say about Joseph: "Because the patriarchs [Joseph's brothers] were jealous of Joseph, they sold him as a slave into Egypt. But God was with him and rescued him from all his troubles" (Acts 7:9-10). Years after being betrayed by his brothers, Joseph's presence in Egypt saved his whole family from starvation. Did jealousy, then, bring about something good? Not really. *God* brought about something good, in spite of jealousy.

Similarly, when the Jewish priests turned Jesus over to Pilate, offering trumped-up charges, even Pilate recognized their blatant jealousy: "he knew it was out of envy that they had handed Jesus over to him" (Mt 27:18). Those actions, motivated by jealousy, were used by God to bring about our redemption through the death of Jesus. It is good—to say the least—to know that God will work through me and in spite of me, even if I am jealous. It is also good to know that our God is a forgiving God.

Our third reason for hope in the face of jealousy is that *God is full of grace*. When I sin, I usually try to ignore it at first. Then as God's Spirit presses conviction upon me, I confess my sin. And, in the name of Jesus, my sin is forgiven. But it often continues to haunt me. If someone else has seen me sin, then embarrassment may haunt me too. If no one "caught" me, still guilt may haunt me, because I know God saw. Since jealousy is usually a private, silent sin, its companion may be guilt. Even if no one else knows, how can God accept me when I have been so sinful?

It is not because I have conquered my jealousy that God accepts me. My relationship with God is based on the cross of Jesus. My sins are forgiven because Jesus died for me. Because of his death, I can confess my jealousy and be at peace with God. In confession we are saying that we agree with God about the sinfulness of our deed or thought. In confession we ask that he forgive us, not because we deserve it, but simply because he is merciful and forgiving: "as far as the east is from the west, so far has he removed our transgressions from us" (Ps 103:12). "If we confess our sins, he is faithful and just and will forgive us our sins and purify us from all unrighteousness" (1 Jn 1:9).

As our daughters were growing up, there were many times when they disobeyed me. Their disobedience made me very sad, and sometimes very mad! But after the reprimand or correction, there would often be tears and reconciliation. As my little girl climbed up in my lap to snuggle in for a hug, I can remember thinking, "Oh! I love her so much! Now what was it I was angry about?" I couldn't remember my anger because my love was even stronger. "How much more will your Father in heaven give good gifts to those who ask him!" (Mt 7:11). As I dried my daughter's tears, I would often think of God's promise to one day dry all of my own tears. "The Sovereign LORD will wipe away the tears from all faces; he will remove the disgrace of his people from all the earth" (Is 25:8).

We do not, then, need to be afraid of our sin, even if our sin is a silent sin like jealousy. Our hope, ultimately, is in God's sovereign mercy. Jealousy and envy, like all sin, need not overwhelm us.

In fact, God will do even more than forgive our sin. He will also cleanse the rot. I found that out the day I first saw Sheila's house. It was indeed a rotten day, but eventually I confessed my sin of jealousy. I told God that I really did appreciate the house he had given me. There are even some advantages to a smaller house! I confessed that I had ignored his love for me by focusing on what he had given Sheila. I asked him to change my heart. And he did. Today, years later, I am particularly grateful that God gave me the courage to face my jealousy, because Sheila is still my friend. I visit her often. And I can honestly say that I harbor no jealousy when I walk through her front door. This small miracle, concerning a relatively insignificant detail of life, reminds me how much God loves me and how much he cares about my struggles and my victories.

Scripture for Reflection or Discussion

1. "A heart at peace gives life to the body, but envy rots the bones" (Prov 14:30).
   When are you most at "peace" in your relationships with those close to you? How does that peace affect your body? In contrast, what effect does envy have on you?

2. "The Word became flesh and made his dwelling among us. We have seen his glory, the glory of the One and Only, who came from the Father, full of grace and truth" (Jn 1:14).
   Think about one or two experiences you have had with jealousy. If you were having a conversation with Jesus about these experiences, what do you think he would say about *grace* and your jealousy? About *truth* and your jealousy? What difference would it make in your life today if you allowed yourself to

experience more of Jesus' grace and truth?

3. "What shall we say, then? Shall we go on sinning so that grace may increase?" (Rom 6:1).

This question, raised by the apostle Paul, reflects a question some of us may be honest enough to ask: "If God is gracious and forgiving in the face of my jealousy, and if he is going to accomplish his purposes anyway, why bother trying to overcome my jealous inclinations?"

Paul answers his own question in the next verse: "By no means!" How would you answer this question? Support your answer with evidence from your own life.

3

If God Can Be Jealous, Why Can't I?

I *have often wondered what it* sounded like when God spoke to the Israelites. Did he speak in actual words? Did his voice sound like thunder? Or did he speak only through human beings, telling them exactly what he wanted them to say?

Whatever it sounded like, we do know for certain what the Israelites heard. At one point in their march across the desert they heard these words: "I, the LORD your God, am a jealous God" (Ex 20:5)!

Later, Moses said it again: "The LORD, whose name is Jealous, is a jealous God" (Ex 34:14). God felt emotions generated by jealousy: "By the sins they committed they stirred up his jealous anger" (1 Kings 14:22). Jealousy is even part of God's love: "Then the LORD will be jealous for his land and take pity on his people" (Joel 2:18). Paul wrote that he, a human being, shared in God's jealousy: "I am jealous for you with a godly jealousy" (2 Cor 11:2).

So what's going on here? Why is it good for God to be jealous, but a sin for us to be jealous? Why did Paul sound almost proud of his jealousy?

The answer to these questions lies in the meaning of the Greek and Hebrew words translated *jealousy*. My theological dictionaries tell me that the Hebrew word *qinnē'* and the Greek word *zēloō* can both be translated "to be jealous of" or "to be zealous for." "The distinction is not in the term. Instead it is found in the relationship of the person to the thing that is desired."[1] The Greek word can be defined as "an emotional going out to a person, idea, or cause."[2] When the goal is good, the word means "eager striving, competition, enthusiasm, admiration." When the goal is sinful, the word means "jealousy, ill-will, or envy."[3] The sin of jealousy, then, reflects self-centeredness—desiring something that is not rightfully ours. In contrast, the godly form of jealousy points to a desire which is good because it contributes to life as God intends for it to be.

God's Jealous Love for Us

When God calls himself jealous, then, he is saying that he is reaching out to us, that he passionately wants to claim us for himself. We were created to live in the center of his love. Every act of disobedience takes us away from that center, takes us into dangerous territory where we forget that he loves us, where we think we can and should control our own lives, where we risk using relationships to serve ourselves instead of our Creator.

As we begin to move toward that place of alienation from God's love, his Spirit jealously hovers over our spirits, making

us uncomfortable, trying to turn our hearts back to our Lord.
God is jealous when anything in our lives deters us from resting
in his love. His Spirit is jealous when I begin to think that I
cannot get along without more money, a larger house, a better
job or a different body. His Spirit is jealous when I think that
I deserve the honor another person is getting, or when I am
ambitious to achieve anything but his will. His Spirit is jealous
when my motivation is anything but love. My money, my house,
my body, my career, my achievements all belong to God.

God's jealousy, then, actually grows out of his love. Because
he loves us, he is jealous of anything that might tempt us away
from what is good for us. It might be similar to a loving father
whose teenage daughter has fallen head over heels in love with
a young man who is into drugs. If the father is jealous of that
young man, his jealousy reflects God's jealousy. Because he
loves her, he wants the best for his daughter. The anxiety he
feels as he sees the unhealthy relationship develop is godly
jealousy.

Suppose, however, that another father's love for his daughter
is diluted with his own selfish ambition. In fact, let's make it
even more complicated. This father is a missionary and the
child of missionaries. In the tradition of his family, he always
expected his own children to serve God on the mission field.
Meanwhile, his daughter, away at college, falls in love with an
engineer who is a Christian but who has no sense of God's call
to the mission field. Dad finds himself jealous of his daughter's
relationship with the young engineer. Is this godly jealousy or
sinful jealousy? Only the dad knows for sure. If he is free to be
honest with himself, he may find himself admitting that he is
worried about what his family will think—his only daughter
entering the world of corporate America! Or perhaps his honesty will lead him to realize that he had hoped his daughter

would continue his own work, maybe even making up for some of his failures. Enter sinful jealousy. Sinful jealousy is the cause of the anxiety we feel when we fear we are losing something which would make us look better or feel better about ourselves, whether it is God's will for us or not.

Complaining to God

Another way to look at sinful jealousy is to consider the possibility that *when I am jealous, I am complaining.* I am complaining to God that I do not have all that I should have. I am telling God that I know what I need better than he does. The difference between sinful jealousy and godly jealousy is that sinful jealousy is focused on my needs and desires rather than on God's sovereign love. This is not to say that it is wrong to want things or that we should not admit our needs and desires. But when they begin to grip at our gut, then we have probably given in to jealousy.

This gut-gripping, jealous anxiety may lead us to act in foolish and self-serving ways. Our attempts to get out from under this anxiety may cause us to sin. At first, we may actually enjoy the results of our sin: the coveted promotion we manipulated our way into, the new possession we bought, the sought-after honor we wangled. But eventually, as we experience jealousy again and again, the pain it causes may lead us back to God.

That's right. Sometimes even our jealousy itself leads us back to God. Paul wrote that God's intent was to make his own people, the Israelites, jealous by giving salvation to the Gentiles. Perhaps then the Israelites would return to God. Paul said that the sin of the Israelites did not damage them beyond repair, that jealousy was the tool God used to try to bring them back to himself. "Did they [the Israelites] stumble so as to fall beyond recovery? Not at all! Rather, because of their transgression, salvation has come to the Gentiles to make Israel envious" (Rom 11:11). Perhaps in their envy of the Gentiles the Israelites would return to God.

Whenever jealousy causes us to sharpen our own desire to obey the Lord God, or whenever jealousy leads us to repentance and reordering of our priorities, then the weapon which was in Satan's hands has been given back to God.

The Place of the Mind

The key to whether our jealousy leads to repentance or to more sin has to do with our *thoughts,* not our feelings. We cannot "unfeel" our feelings. By the time we know they are there, we have already felt them. In fact, God seems to be persistently unembarrassed by the *feelings* of his people. Scripture tells us that God's people have experienced all kinds of feelings that many people would consider "unacceptable." They have hated (Ps 139:19-22). They have wanted to die (1 Kings 19:4). They have wanted to sin (Rom 7:18-21). They have certainly been jealous.

But the problem is not with the feelings themselves. Our feelings are a source of information about ourselves. They are a God-given tool to help us understand ourselves and our relationships with others. That is why we should not ignore them. One of the things our feelings may tell us is that something is wrong with the way we are looking at our lives. (If, for instance, I feel that I am always a failure, it may be because I am thinking that I need to do everything perfectly.) We cannot control the feelings that seem to enter our hearts uninvited. But we can influence the way we think. Often as our thinking changes, our feelings will change too.

Even if our feelings do not change, we can use our mental capacities to motivate our wills. This is why Scripture tells us to be "transformed" by the renewing of our minds (Rom 12:2).

Paul said that he wanted to "take captive every thought to make it obedient to Christ" (2 Cor 10:5). One of the best weapons we have against jealousy is our brain. We can choose to believe Satan, who is a liar, or we can choose to believe God, who says that he loves us and will not withhold anything good from us (Ps 84:11).

Please do not misunderstand me. I am not saying that our thoughts are more godly than our feelings. Scripture does not teach that. It is when we use our thoughts and our feelings in tandem that we benefit most from both of them. I do not usually decide with my thoughts to feel something. My feelings, rather, are a spontaneous response to what I think. Because they are spontaneous, they may give me very helpful information. For example, they may tell me something is important to me which I had not recognized before. They may tell me I am afraid of something I did not know I feared. They may actually help me understand what I really think about life. Jealousy is a feeling which may help me know what I think about God, myself and others.

The day I was jealous of Sheila's house, Satan was whispering to me through my own desires and greed, "God must love Sheila more than you. Look at the house he gave her. And other people must think she is really special to live in such a lovely home. You—you live in a raised ranch. Just a regular raised ranch." Except for the fact that our house is a raised ranch, those words were all lies. A house does not make a person special. And God does not love one of his children more than another. I know that. But my jealous heart wanted to believe Satan. It took discipline to stop listening to Satan and my feelings and to start listening to God and my thoughts. I had to *stop* and *think* about the *truth* of the situation before my jealousy began to dissipate.

A Practical Approach

When I was on staff with InterVarsity, I was invited to be part of a small discussion group with a well-known theologian. We sat in an apartment living room, lounging on "early attic" furniture, discussing large faith issues. At one point, I asked with some frustration, "So what is 'faith'?" The eminent gray-haired scholar answered me with an observation that changed my life. "Faith," he said, "is thinking about God and applying what you know about God to the situation at hand." That comment has been one of the building blocks of my spiritual life for the last twenty-five years.

It is an observation that can be helpful to us as we look at this issue of jealousy. When I struggle with jealousy, or any other sin or temptation, I can ask myself, "What do I know about God, and how can I apply that information to this situation?" What does the Bible say about who God is? How have I seen God work in my life in the past? What have others told me about how he works in their lives? How does all this information about God apply to these circumstances in my life right now where I am experiencing jealousy? As I think about God in this way, I sometimes find my spirit lifted to praise him for his goodness. Other times I find myself called to repentance as I realize that I have forgotten who he really is.

In my own life, when I struggle with jealousy, I often forget that God loves me and that he is a sovereign, all-powerful Person. When I am jealous, I am apt to think that God loves someone else more than me. Recalling what I know about God often reminds me that my jealousy is rooted in the arrogant assumption that I could do a better job than God in this business of loving! In light of my jealousy, God's Spirit may remind me that I am not God. I do not always know what is best for me or for others, and even if I did know, I could not always make good happen. Underneath my jealousy is sinful pride.

Who Do You Think You Are?

Job, the famous suffering patriarch of the Old Testament, also had to face his pride. Job suffered more in a few years than I will in a lifetime. Job's problem was not primarily jealousy, but I find that as God challenges my arrogance and jealousy, he sometimes speaks to me with the same sad, ironic words he used with Job:

Where were you when I laid the earth's foundation?

Tell me, if you understand. . . .

Have you ever given orders to the morning,

or shown the dawn its place,

that it might take the earth by the edges

and shake the wicked out of it? . . .

Do you know when the mountain goats give birth?

Do you watch when the doe bears her fawn? . . .

Does the eagle soar at your command

and build his nest on high? . . .

Will the one who contends with the Almighty correct him?

Let him who accuses God answer him! (Job 38:4, 12-13; 39:1, 27; 40:2)

God, whose name is Jealous, looks at my jealousy and says, in effect, "Who do you think you are?"

Like Job, I must answer, "I am unworthy—how can I reply to you? I put my hand over my mouth" (Job 40:4). No words can defend my jealousy. God, who made everything, loves me. That fact alone takes the backbone out of my jealousy. All that I am and have was created by a God who loves me and offers me everything I need that is good and necessary for my life (Ps 84:11; 2 Pet 1:3). Who am I to say that I do not have what I need, or that I deserve to get everything I want, or that I need what someone else has? "Surely I spoke of things I did not understand. . . . My ears had heard of you but now my eyes have seen you. Therefore I . . . repent" (Job 42:3, 5-6).

Faith and repentance, then, are the goals as we examine our sinful jealousy. When we really see God, with the eyes of our spirits, we will know that he has indeed given us all that we need for life and godliness. We will know that he loves us and cares for us better than we could ever care for ourselves. The very fact that God is jealous makes it unnecessary for us to be jealous. God is already jealous for us. He is jealous about anything which would not be good for us, whether it "feels" good now or not. And since he is Creator, King, Lord, and Father of all, I do not need to bother being jealous for myself.

But this is easier said than done! I moan, with Paul, "I have the desire to do what is good, but I cannot carry it out" (Rom 7:18). I may agree that faith and repentance are the best response to jealousy, but I cannot keep the jealous thoughts from entering my head! Jealousy is like a great, powerful beast. It attacks me when I least suspect it is there. I hate it. And yet, I admit, sometimes I invite it. I invite this beast to sit at my table and commiserate with me in my pain and self-pity.

Is there any way to kill this beast, who is sometimes my guest? Probably not. We cannot, once and for all, kill any sin. But we can subdue it. We can learn its scent and flee from it. We can learn its tactics and outfox it. And we can learn our own vulnerabilities to its lure—and work at strengthening those weak areas.

God has not left us defenseless against this beast of jealousy. As we look more closely at what jealousy is, how it traps us and what emotions it camouflages, we can learn to live our lives by faith and not by selfish desires. As with any temptation to sin, there is a way of escape. "No temptation has seized you except what is common to man. And God is faithful; he will not let you be tempted beyond what you can bear. But when you are tempted, he will also provide a way out so that you can stand up under it" (1 Cor 10:13).

Our jealousy will not win. With God's help we can learn to overcome temptation and find freedom to love and be loved.

Scripture for Reflection or Discussion

1. "Proclaim this word: This is what the LORD Almighty says: 'I am very jealous for Jerusalem and Zion' " (Zech 1:14).

How does it make you feel to think that God may be jealous for you? Does that jealousy seem like an expression of love or of anger? Why? What activities, attitudes or relationships in your life might provoke God's jealousy?

2. "As obedient children, do not conform to the evil desires you had when you lived in ignorance" (1 Pet 1:14).

If you remember the time before you became a Christian, write down some of the desires you had then. Write down some of the desires you have today. Now write down some of the desires you wish you had or you think God wants you to have. Put an x by the desires you would like to let go. Put a * by the desires you would like to encourage. What means do you think God is most likely to use to change your desires? How will changing your desires change the ways you relate to other people, especially any tendencies you have toward jealousy?

3. "You were taught, with regard to your former way of life, to put off your old self, which is being corrupted by its deceitful desires; to be made new in the attitude of your minds; and to put on the new self, created to be like God in true righteousness and holiness" (Eph 4:22-24).

Why is this an important Christian teaching? In your own experience, which is most likely to change first, your mind or your feelings? Which do you like better, your mind or your feelings? How do your thoughts affect your feelings? How do your feelings affect your thoughts?

4

Why Am I Jealous When I Don't Want to Be?

The wedding was glorious. People came from all over the country to celebrate. Our church sanctuary looked like a spring garden, with an arbor made of lilies, azaleas and roses. The bride and groom were a handsome couple, delighted in their love for one another and thrilled that the day for their union in marriage had finally arrived. Everyone there was happy for them.

Except me. I was jealous. The bride was one of my best friends. For fifteen years we had shared our lives, our secrets, our aspirations. She had been an intimate part of our lives, moving with us from New Hampshire to Wisconsin, being a friend to our daughters as they grew from toddler days to young womanhood. We had shared meals, ministry, church, even some vacations, for well over a decade. Now, on the day of her marriage, on the day of all days when I should "rejoice with those who rejoice," I was jealous.

I was jealous of the groom. Who did he think he was to take my friend away from me, carrying her off to Texas, surely the other side of the world? I was jealous of her family. What right did they have to arrive here in our city, decorate our church, rent "our" restaurant and, most of all, act as though they knew her better than I did? I was even jealous of the wedding party—including Bob and our girls! Why were they allowed to be together in the bride's parlor while I sat out in the sanctuary waiting for the music to begin?

These thoughts shocked me. How could I feel this way? For a while, I pretended I was happy. Then I bumped into another good friend. She looked at me with an understanding smile. My pretense fell away as tears filled my eyes and I confessed, "I am so sad today!"

It took a while (days, in fact) to realize that what I perceived as jealousy was, in truth, grief. My jealous feelings were actually a camouflage for even more painful feelings. If I was jealous, I could blame other people for what they were doing to me. If I was sad, I would need to face and feel my grief alone. My grief was certainly not the grief of death, but I was grieving a tremendous loss, the loss of our friendship as we had known it. We would need to rebuild our friendship under a different set of circumstances. We would do that. But in the meantime, I needed to grieve the loss of a relationship that was very important to me. And in order to work through that grief, I needed to let go of my jealousy.

Letting go involved asking myself several questions. When I put my mind in gear to do that, I saw how ridiculous my jealousy had been. Was I really jealous that my friend was getting married? Her husband is the answer to my prayers as well as hers for her life partner. I couldn't ask for a better husband for her. No, I'm not really jealous of their marriage.

Was I really jealous of the bride's family? No, I guess not. They have, after all, known her for longer than I have. Besides, they are nice people. I like them. And she has enough love to go around to us all.

How about the wedding party? Was I really jealous of them? Well, maybe a little. I really did want to be where the action was before the ceremony. But both my daughters and my husband were part of the wedding party. And did I really want to walk down the aisle as a bridesmaid? Not on your life! No, I said to myself, what I felt that day was not primarily jealousy.

Without the camouflage of jealousy, I had to face the pain of my grief. And grief is very painful. All I could do was to allow myself to be sad, to cry, to hurt. There were moments when I actually felt the physical pain of grief. I needed to let myself feel that. Eventually, the healing process began, because God did not design us to live forever in grief.

That wedding day reminded me again that we may use our own jealousy—which is real, unpleasant and difficult—as a camouflage for some other emotion, sin or misconception which we refuse to admit. This could be grief, anger, fear—anything which we wish we were not feeling. Or it could be a camouflage for a personal assumption that we wish we didn't have.

I may *say* that I believe God is omnipotent but *live* under the assumption that I need to be constantly on guard against physical and psychological harm. If something or someone threatens me, I may use jealousy to avoid facing my false assumption. (To a certain extent, my jealousy at the wedding grew out of my false assumption that I have to be needed in order to be loved, so I was jealous of those who were needed more than I was that day.) In some perverse way, it may feel safer to be jealous than to deal with my fear that God will not help me when I hurt, or that he does not care about what I think I need. Or perhaps I allow myself to be jealous in situations where I am afraid that if I look twice, I might see that I am really questioning the essence of God's love for me.

Remember that the dictionary said jealousy is feeling resentful about another person's success or advantages. It is a suspicion or fear of rivalry. Envy is a feeling of discontent about another person's superiority. Notice that these feelings all focus on other people. If we are honest with ourselves, most of us would say that it is easier to talk about someone else's faults than our own. Well-known historian Will Durant said that "criticizing others is a dishonest way of praising ourselves." It would not be too far-fetched to say that jealousy of others is a dishonest way of excusing ourselves. Or, dare we say it? Jealousy may be a dishonest way of criticizing God for not giving us what we want.

The problem with all of this is that when I do not admit the real problem (an inaccurate view of myself, God or my friend), I work very hard to avoid a confrontation with the truth. I become so busy focusing on why life is unfair, why someone else is getting what I deserve, or why I should be able to do what someone else does, that I no longer have the emotional energy to believe God or to love other people. It is exceedingly difficult to love someone who arouses my jealousy. If I can somehow understand and deal with the jealousy, then my heart will be freer to love.

Right and Wrong Jealousy

Jealousy is almost always multilayered. Underneath the top layer, the raw feelings of jealousy, there will probably be several other thoughts and feelings which we need to examine. Sometimes we will find disbelief or other sin. Sometimes we will find 'd personal wounds. Sometimes we will discover spiritual and notional work which we need to do. And, of course, sometimes e will find godliness, when our jealousy reflects God's jealsy. But the raw jealousy may *feel* the same, regardless of hat is underneath. It takes God-given discernment to determine whether our jealousy is rooted in something good, something that needs healing or something that is essentially sinful. This struggle is not a twentieth-century phenomenon. oses, some 3,300 years ago, spoke to husbands, telling them hat to do if any one of them felt jealousy in his marriage (Num 11-30). If a man was jealous because he thought his wife had een unfaithful, and if she was in fact involved in an adulterous lationship, then his jealousy was "good" jealousy, because od agreed with him about the value of marital faithfulness. ut suppose the wife had not been unfaithful at all, yet the usband was still filled with suspicious, jealous rage. How uld he, or anyone, know the difference between righteous alousy and unrighteous jealousy?

The rage that the husband felt might be similar to the strong elings we feel when we think we have been deprived of mething we deserve. Even if our jealousy is ill-founded, as e husband's might have been, the feelings run deep and can erwhelm us. How are we to know which kind of jealousy we re experiencing? There are certainly times when our jealous elings may be as godly as the jealousy of a husband whose ife has been unfaithful. If I am jealous, for instance, of meone in the office who gets a promotion because of blatant, ishonest flattery, then my jealous feeling may actually reflect e anger of God toward deceit. Or if a single woman is jealous f a neighbor who enjoys the attention of an attractive man in change for the favors of her body, then the young woman's alousy may be rooted in God's high standards of morality.

Feelings which we call jealousy may actually be feelings of grief that sin has destroyed part of God's plan for his creation. But those feelings probably feel about the same as the jealous feelings which, in truth, reflect our own selfishness or unbelief. The office worker and the young woman may also be jealous because it looks to their unbelieving eyes as if God is allowing someone else to have what they themselves cannot get.

So how *can* we tell the difference?

I know better than anyone else that my heart is "deceitful above all things" (Jer 17:9). Give me the slightest excuse for jealousy and my heart will snatch it up right away! Of course I would rather say that my feelings reflect God's distaste for flattery and immorality than admit that I think God is unfair!

This masquerade of good jealousy and sinful jealousy was so difficult for the Israelites that God gave Moses a "law of jealousy," actually a test used to discover the truth of the situation. I wish I could say that Moses' law, or test, could be helpful to us, but it is a strange law indeed! It is rooted in customs foreign to us, in a patriarchal tradition that would be offensive today. The husband was to take his wife and a sacrifice to the priest, and the priest was to perform a ritualistic test on the woman to see whether she was guilty or not. Even though the test itself is extremely culture-bound, we learn from Numbers 5 that God takes our problem seriously and recognizes that sometimes our jealousy will confuse us. No matter what the variations of our society, the human heart needs help in understanding its own motives and desires.

A Test of Jealousy

Following Moses' example, I wonder if we could come up with a "test of jealousy" which would help us untangle our own twentieth-century experiences with jealousy. No test, definition or formula will work equally well in every situation, but perhaps we could start with our definition of faith: Faith is thinking about God and applying what you know about God to the situation at hand. Add to that a similar definition of jealousy: Jealousy is thinking about another person and wishing you had what that person has. The test of jealousy, then, might be a question: *Is this thing (possession, attribute, honor) something which God wants me to have at this time, and is it something which I can attain in a way that honors him?*

Judy is a friend of mine who is working on her doctorate at the University of Wisconsin. Steve is a friend of ours who received his doctorate six months ago. Was Judy jealous at Steve's celebration party? You bet she was! Was her jealousy sin? Probably not. Only Judy knows for sure. She wished she had *her* doctorate already, and she said she was jealous of Steve, but rather than complain, she went back to her computer and started working harder on her thesis.

I have another friend, Brent, who is the quiet, intellectual type. Brent was jealous when his coworker Allen received a promotion. Unlike Brent, Allen has a forceful, aggressive personality. Was Brent's jealousy sin? Possibly. The temptation to jealousy, of course, is not sin, but as Brent found himself wallowing in self-pity, he probably forgot that it was God who created each human being with a unique temperament. Brent found himself focusing on Allen's faults, on all the reasons why he should not have received the promotion. Needless to say, as jealousy tightened its grip, Brent found it hard to love Allen.

You and I both know that Judy and Brent's struggles look minor only with objective hindsight. At the time, for each of them, the struggle was with raw jealousy. They both had to decide what to do with their jealousy, in light of who God is and what he desired for them as individuals. When Judy looked underneath her jealousy, she knew that the only answer was to return to her computer. When Brent examined his jealousy, he went to his knees in prayer, confessing that he was angry with God for not giving him a charismatic personality. He asked God to help him love and affirm Allen in spite of his temptation to jealousy. Both Brent and Judy had a lot of work left to do. But at least they were taking steps to avoid wasting more time being jealous.

The law, or test, of jealousy, then, might tell me to come before the Lord my God and ask him if he wants me to have what it is that I desire. I can ask him to allow me to see the manifestation of his love in my life. I can confess to him that I do not want my focus to be on anyone else. I want to understand his call to *me*.

Dealing Directly with God

Jealousy makes a triangle out of my relationship with God. Instead of relating to God directly, as Jesus' death allows me to, I filter my relationship with him through the shadow of what I perceive as someone else's relationship with him. I tell God that I will love him more (or he will love me more) if he gives me the same advantages someone else has. The test of jealousy takes away that filter. I come to God openly and honestly and ask him about my concerns. Do I need what I think I need? May I have what I think I want? Are my desires biblical or self-serving? Can I fulfill them in a righteous, loving way, or will I have to selfishly promote myself? Do my desires need to be fulfilled immediately or does God want me to wait? If I take the time to ask these questions, using them as a test of jealousy, they will soften the lure of my neighbor's advantages or gifts. If God wants to give me what my neighbor has, fine. If not, fine. I need to remember that my neighbor has his or her unique relationship to the Lord and I have mine.

When Peter began to wonder about the future of his fellow disciple John, he asked Jesus, "Lord, what about him?" Jesus' reply was, "What is that to you? You must follow me" (Jn 21:21-22). In the final analysis, my jealousy becomes irrelevant because I must follow Jesus alone. Jesus has some "good works" planned for me to do (Eph 2:8-9). Whenever I focus on someone else's works or looks or talents, I waste energy that could be used for what the Lord has in mind for me.

When It Won't Go Away

But suppose I apply the law of jealousy to my situation and nothing changes. Before God I have asked myself all the appropriate questions. I've decided that my jealousy is ill-founded, and I am determined not to be jealous any more. But *I am still jealous.*

This may be an indication of something going on inside of me which I need to correct or an area where I need to be healed. Look again at the husband in Moses' camp. Suppose he found out from the priest that his wife was not guilty of adultery. Presumably, he could go home and live happily ever after. But jealousy does not always let go so easily. If that man lived in our time, he might struggle with fear every time his wife worked late, worrying that she was with another man. Or he might bristle whenever his wife talked with a male friend at a party. Even after applying the test of jealousy, the husband might still struggle with jealous feelings.

A military term describes what might be going on in this situation. It fits with the idea that jealousy may be a camou-flage. The word is *camouflet.* A camouflet is "an underground explosion of a bomb or mine that does not break the surface, but leaves an enclosed cavity of gas or smoke; or the pocket formed by such an explosion."[1] It may be that a childhood wound or a large adult disappointment was inadvertently buried within us, deep within our subconscious. Whatever caused that wound or disappointment may have been like an explosion within us, leaving a cavity. Into the cavity rushes not smoke but jealousy. The husband's jealousy (or my jealousy, or your jealousy) may actually come out of the camouflet, rather than out of current events.

When we experience jealous feelings that are not related to the truth of the situation or to the truth we know about God, we may need to look within ourselves and see if there is a camouflet hidden there, causing us the anxiety we feel. In the cavity of the camouflet there may be some grains of truth. (Yes, some wives are unfaithful.) And there will most likely be some hurt. (Yes, what happened to me in the past hurt me deeply, and I never want to experience that kind of hurt again.) But as we look at the hurt of the past, we may be able to see how our current jealous feelings are really a camouflage, reflecting something other than the reality of our situation today.

Just as it usually takes military experts to deal with camouflets, it usually takes other people—trained counselors or gifted friends—to deal with the emotional camouflets of our lives. It is not easy to ask for help in dealing with the emotional wounds of our past. But all of this is a part of growth, spiritual as well as emotional. And all of us need to grow, whatever the hidden perils of our lives.

Paul said, "Not that I . . . have already been made perfect, but I press on. . . . Forgetting what is behind and straining toward what is ahead, I press on toward the goal to win the prize for which God has called me heavenward in Christ Jesus. . . . If on some point you think differently, that too God will make clear to you. Only let us live up to what we have already attained" (Phil 3:12-16). We have none other than the great Counselor himself on our side.

Scripture for Reflection or Discussion

1. "All a man's ways seem innocent to him, but motives are weighed by the LORD" (Prov 16:2). "He [the Lord] will bring to light what is hidden in darkness and will expose the motives of men's hearts" (1 Cor 4:5).

Does it reassure you or frighten you to think that God knows your motives? When have you experienced jealousy that grew out of selfish motives on your part? What effect did your jealousy have on the relationship? What did you do about it?

2. "You adulterous people, don't you know that friendship with the world is hatred toward God?" (Jas 4:4).

You probably do not consider yourself an adulterer, but think honestly for a moment about areas in your life where you "flirt" with the world. What values of your culture are very important to you, whether they are Christian values or not? What do you do to try to gain these things for yourself? How can you tell if you are just flirting with the world or actually committing adultery, giving yourself up to those values?

3. "Forgetting what is behind and straining toward what is ahead, I press on toward the goal to win the prize for which God has called me" (Phil 3:13-14).

What negative attitude do you want to let go, to leave behind you? What is the prize to which you are called? Do you like that prize? Why or why not? What can you do today to press on toward that prize, moving in faith and grace rather than fear and guilt?

5

Wishful Thinking

*P**aul was mad. The Christians* in the new church at Corinth were acting like a bunch of babies, still on a diet of milk and pabulum. He wrote to the brothers and sisters there, "I could not address you as spiritual but as worldly—mere infants in Christ. I gave you milk, not solid food, for you were not yet ready for it. Indeed, you are still not ready. You are still worldly. For since there is jealousy and quarreling among you, are you not worldly?" (1 Cor 3:1-3).

Do you know what the Corinthians were fighting about? They were jealous and quarreling about who belonged to what clique. Some said, "I follow Paul." Others lifted their chins in arrogance and said, "Well, I follow Apollos!" Just like children in a schoolyard at recess. Five or six little girls run off and separate themselves from the others to form a "club," designed to make them feel superior to their fellow classmates. Or perhaps it is a special "team" of little boys which includes only the very best athletes.

No wonder Paul could not teach the Corinthians deep spiritual truths. They were too busy protecting the image they had
created for themselves or worrying about being left out of the
group they perceived as most special. At the root of these
preoccupations was immaturity—and its symptom was jealousy.

In our own struggles with jealousy, it might help to pick up
on Paul's idea that jealousy is a form of immaturity. What is
immaturity? What differentiates children from adults? What
does childish thinking look like? Immature thinking is self-centered, impatient and unrealistic. All of these things feed into
jealous feelings.

Self-Centered

Childish, immature thinking is, first of all, self-centered. Newborn babies have almost no awareness of the world around
them. Their life revolves around food, wakefulness and sleep.
They are completely dependent on what others give them—un-
able to provide for themselves and unaware of what they can
give to other people. When we get stuck in the journey from
infancy to adulthood, we remain childish and selfish.

Jealousy, like immaturity, is childish and selfish. It assumes
that the world owes us something—honor, money, affirmation.
It is self-conscious and assumes that the world is paying more
attention than it is. Rather than looking at the world from the
vantage point of the Father's love and the Creator's plan,
jealousy looks at the world through selfish eyes (am I getting
what I want? am I getting what I think I deserve?). Jealousy
touches our lives in places where immaturity makes us particularly vulnerable. When jealousy sees a spot in my life where
I am acting self-centered and immature, it rushes in and
whispers, "You deserve better than that."

"I Want It Now!"

Jealousy is also impatient. A hungry baby screams in frustration until milk calms the hunger pangs. In our most jealous moments, we cry out in immaturity, "I want what I want and I want it now!"

We live in an impatient world. We don't like to wait. If I miss the left-turn signal at an intersection near my home, I have to wait fifty-five seconds for the green arrow to come again (I've timed it). Sometimes that irritates me.

Television promises me instantaneous pleasure if I buy the right products. It also promises thirty-minute solutions to most problems, no matter what their cause. We impatiently get rid of anything we don't like as soon as possible. We have climate control, sound control, even smell control. We will not tolerate the unpleasant. It simply must not be. Time-consuming growth is ignored. There are trees inside the mall where only a barren field existed last year. I can make life all I want it to be. If I can't do it for myself, I'll find someone else to do it for me. And if I have my way, it won't take very long.

I want what I want—so badly that the minute someone else gets it, envy is triggered in me. Life tricked me. A promise was made, but the goods were delivered to someone else. I deserve better than that.

Make-Believe Thinking

The promise "You can have whatever you want in life" is, of course, a lie. But in my moments of immaturity, I believe the lie is true. Immaturity is not only self-centered and impatient, it is also unrealistic. This is probably the one characteristic of immaturity which does the most damage in our relationships. And it is one which clearly fosters jealousy.

Young children are often totally unrealistic in their view of the world. The other day I overheard a little girl in a restaurant tell her mother that she wanted to fly. Her mother convinced her that she would be able to fly better after she ate her pancakes! That kind of pretend play is fun for children. But it is not fun when adults believe lies about relationships and about life. Psychologists call this kind of unrealistic thinking denial.

With children we expect some denial: "Johnny, did you spill the milk?" "Oh, no, Mommy, the cat did it." But denial is a different story twenty years later: "John, haven't you already had one drink too many?" "Oh, get off my back! I can handle it!" Later, John's wife may play into denial in their marriage: "This black eye? Oh, John accidentally hit me last night. It's nothing." We become adept at denying things we wish were not true about the ones we love. An abused wife will often deny the truth about her bruises.

This kind of I-wish-it-weren't-true thinking plays right into the camouflage of jealousy. Kay wishes she weren't angry that the boss likes Suzanne better than he likes her. So she becomes jealous rather than angry. "Angry? No, I'm not angry. I just don't think it's fair that Suzanne got the promotion."

Or Pastor Smith doesn't understand why Pastor Jones's church is growing by leaps and bounds when he himself has prayed his heart out for new members and gotten very few. It is untenable for him to think that God has answered Pastor Jones's prayers and not his own. Rather than acknowledge a theology-threatening possibility, he denies it and become jealous. "I really don't see what they get out of his sermons. Mine are much better. It must be because he is so tall and good-looking."

Denial, then, is not just the experience of the alcoholic or the abused wife. I do not want to be less successful than others, so I deny their success by jealously criticizing their behavior. And perhaps I do not even want to be jealous, so I ignore jealousy and become superficial, analytical and unfeeling instead.

We may end up putting our arms around Suzanne or Pastor Jones and pretending to love them, while we ache inside. There is nothing wrong with reaching out to love someone even when we don't feel like it. What's wrong is when we deny the truth about our anger, our doubts or our jealousy. Ignoring or denying the truth about what's going on inside eventually distorts our view of our friends and of God. And that's exactly what Satan wants to see happen. Jesus said that our enemy is the father of lies. "When he lies, he speaks his native language" (Jn 8:44). Denial, which cannot or will not acknowledge the truth of a situation, is a weapon that Satan, the great deceiver, uses to destroy loving relationships. The more honest we can be with ourselves, the more equipped we will be to obey Jesus' commandment to love our neighbor. Being honest about my anger and jealousy does not mean that I give in to it. It means that I am *truthful* about it. And the truth sets me free—to let go of myself and to love my neighbor.

Letting Truth In
Let me give an example. One Saturday morning I was cleaning house, dressed in my ever-best cleaning apparel, looking only a little better than I do at my worst. The doorbell rang. It was Marty standing on my doorstep—looking lovely, as always.

Marty had stopped by on her way to a concert to drop off a book she had borrowed from me. I leaned on the vacuum cleaner as we made small talk. Then small talk turned to big talk when Marty mentioned that she was going to the special Saturday concert with Janet. "What! Wait a minute! Janet is *my* friend! Why are you and Janet going without me?"

Of course, I didn't verbalize any of that "big" talk. But I could hardly keep the smile on my face until Marty left. Then I did it. I gave in to jealousy. I launched into the downward spiral. "Why do I have to stay home and clean my house while they go out to lunch and a concert? They probably have cleaning ladies. They probably don't even like me. Look at me—how scruffy can you get? I'm left out. I'm not getting what I deserve." The rot of envy began to set in.

But listen to some of the *truths* my jealousy was denying. First of all, the truth is that I do not have to be invited to every social event my friends go to. Second, even if I wasn't invited because they didn't want me to come, that's okay. My self-worth doesn't depend on their opinion of me. And besides, I may be scruffy, and I may clean my own house, but that's because of choices I've made, and my choices do not always have to be the same ones my friends make.

Finally—and this was the most painful truth—the bottom line, no matter how I said it, was that I had been left out, and that hurt my feelings. But I decided I could handle it. In fact, I decided that I could handle hurt feelings better than jealous feelings. Sometimes my friends will disappoint me, but God has promised never, ever to leave me out.

This conversation with myself sounds childish, doesn't it? Well, it is. Jealousy is childish. And when we take the time to really look at it, we will feel foolish. But it is a good foolishness because it pushes us into the arms of Jesus.

The world says that "trusting Jesus" is a foolish thing to do. It is actually the most honest, healthy thing we can ever do. Paul told the Corinthians that a measure of foolishness was spiritually healthy (1 Cor 1:20-21, 25; 3:18-19). Jealousy says I should be able to have what I want. The world says it is foolish to let go of my desire to promote myself. Jesus says the truth will set me free. My fear says I cannot handle the truth. The truth is that I am not always happy. Sometimes I am jealous of others. I am not always secure. Sometimes I think I need what someone else has. To say the least, I do not like to admit that. But when I admit the truth about my self-centeredness, then I can go home to my heavenly Father. When I am resting in the presence of my Father, I do not need to be self-centered because I remember that he loves me fully and completely, without comparing me to any of his other children.

Let me give one more example that a friend shared with me. This was her own experience. Kristin was falling in love with Eric. Life was wonderful except for one thing. Kristin kept thinking about Eric's former girlfriends. She wondered how she measured up to them. Was she as pretty as they were? Was she as much fun? Did he like her more than he had liked them? Kristin told herself that she was not really jealous, just curious. She sensed that this kind of jealousy could be sinful, so she decided to remain "curious." Of course, she thought she might actually be jealous, but she didn't want to be, so she pretended she wasn't.

The problem with this way of thinking is that it doesn't work. Kristin's "curiosity" was giving her knots in her stomach and anxiety in her relationship with Eric. Finally, when she could stand it no longer, she admitted it: she was jealous. The epistle of James comments that "the spirit he caused to live in us envies intensely" (Jas 4:5). But Kristin found that, as James promises in the next verse, God gives grace. As soon as she admitted her jealousy, God's grace was available to her. She confessed that in her jealousy she was not trusting either Eric or God's love for her. Amazingly, the knots in her stomach left and the anxiety in her heart softened. The truth had set her free. Jesus is the truth that enables us to overcome our denial.

When we look at our lives as objectively as possible, then we can see why Paul was angry with the Corinthians. In their immaturity, they were more interested in self-promotion and self-protection than in truth. The pitted themselves against one another in order to feel good about themselves. They were more adept at jealousy than at love. May God give us the courage to be truthful and loving, to set aside our immaturity and our jealousy. His grace can do that.

Scripture for Reflection or Discussion

1. "Anyone who listens to the word but does not do what it says is like a man who looks at his face in a mirror and, after looking at himself, goes away and immediately forgets what he looks like" (Jas 1:23-24).

   Denial usually involves ignoring something we perceive as negative about ourselves. In what areas of your life do you feel the most uncomfortable? What do you do to try to forget your imperfections in those areas? Are there things you could do, talk about or pray about which would help you be more mature in those areas?

2. Jesus read from the scroll, "The Spirit of the Lord is on me, because he has anointed me to preach good news to the poor. He has sent me to proclaim freedom for the prisoners and recovery of sight for the blind, to release the oppressed, to proclaim the year of the Lord's favor" (Lk 4:18-19).

   In what areas of your life do you feel poor? Imprisoned by emotions or circumstances? Spiritually or relationally blind? Oppressed, by yourself or by others? What effect do these restraints have on your relationships with God and with others? Ask Jesus to give you the freedom he offers here.

3. "They exchanged the truth of God for a lie, and worshiped and served created things rather than the Creator" (Rom 1:25).

   These words describe the godlessness and wickedness of sinful human beings. Christians, even though they have experienced the grace of Jesus, are not immune to the effects of sin. What lies are you tempted to believe which may provoke you to sinful jealousy?

6

Does God Know
That Life Is Unfair?

*W*ho knows what was wrong with him that day? But when I heard him pray, I knew something was bothering him. He sounded angry, almost bitter. I wondered who had stepped on his toes. When he prayed, he said something like this:

God, I just don't understand it. Here I am, trying to love you and serve you, and then you turn around and let people who don't even care about you get the goods. Look at Mike. He doesn't love you the way I do, but he doesn't have half the problems I have. He seems to be above it all, sailing through life without any of the worries of us plebeians. His arrogance makes me sick. He says he's a Christian, but he sure doesn't act like it. And then you bless him. I mean, he is loaded. He doesn't even have to wait for the next paycheck to pay the rent. It makes me think that obeying you doesn't mean

anything. I hate to say it, God. I don't want to discourage
other people, but to be honest, I just don't get it.

Did you recognize these words? I'm not sure I would ever have
the nerve to pray like that in a prayer meeting, but the emotion
running through that prayer has permeated my heart too. I may
not talk about it much, but I agree that sometimes I think God is
royally unfair. I have seen friends be given things that I have to
work hard for. I've known people to be rewarded when they act
in ways that are clearly unbiblical. They get the promotions, the
compliments, the goods. Sometimes it seems it doesn't make any
difference whether I live by kingdom values or not.

But there is another reason why I recognize that prayer. It
is not only written in my heart, it is also written in God's
Word—in Psalm 73. This sad, jealous prayer is a loose para-
phrase of verses 4-16. Once again, I take comfort in the
scriptural evidence that what goes on in my heart does not
surprise God. He knows that life will be unfair. God knows
about the rot of envy which can corrode my heart and mind.
He knows that sometimes, when life seems particularly unfair,
I blame him.

He knows about our jealousy toward one another. Just like
siblings who vie for the attentions and favors of their parents,
we can become childish and critical as we blame each other
and God when we don't get what we want. If we feel too
uncomfortable getting angry with God, we may focus our anger
and jealousy on our brothers and sisters.

We spoke about anger in the last chapter. Let's examine it
more closely. For when we untangle our jealous feelings, more
often than not we will indeed find anger. In fact, anger is such
a common thread of jealousy that I have learned to ask myself,
What are you angry about? almost as soon as I feel jealousy
creep into my heart.

Sometimes I find I am angry about some unrelated event, and my jealousy is almost an excuse to focus my anger in the wrong place. At other times I am angry at God because he seemed not to answer my prayers. Sometimes I am angry at the person who has what I wish I had. But most often, when I look at my anger about a specific thing, I find out that it is part of my larger anger at the unfairness of life.

The Law of Fairness

I tend to live under the assumption that if I act in a certain way, I will get certain results—it's only fair. I also live with the false and sometimes unconscious assumption that everyone should have the same amount of everything, whether it is possessions, opportunities, talents or friends. It's not *fair* that some people have so much and others have so little. That unfairness makes me mad, especially (I admit it) if I am the one on the short end. I believe that our society is moving more and more under the shadow of the assumption that everyone deserves whatever anyone gets.

We believe in the Law of Fairness more than we believe in God.

There is nothing wrong with trying to make life equitable, and there is nothing wrong with being angry when inequality hurts people. I imagine that some of the inequality which makes me angry makes God angry too. But most of my anger about life's unfairness is not righteous anger, reflecting the love of my Father. It is selfish anger, rooted in my desire that God, my friends and my employer be "especially fair" to me. This is the kind of anger which can lead to the bitterness of jealousy. When the sun sets on this kind of anger, the rot of envy can seep into our souls.

Life will always be unfair. My accomplishments will never be satisfactorily affirmed by everyone I know. Someone will always have more than I do. I will always have good reasons to fear that I am missing out on something someone else has. The possibilities are endless. Listen to just a few:

"My raise wasn't as much as Joyce's, and I've worked overtime many more times than she has."

"He was born with a silver spoon in his mouth. His parents bought that house for them. I had to pay for mine with sweat and tears."

"She is so smart she could get into any college. I work my tail off and worry about making it into the local junior college."

"If someone had just noticed me, I could have done that job just as well as he did."

"I had that idea for our church's outreach program three years ago, but nobody listened to me. Now Erin comes along with the same idea and everybody thinks she's wonderful."

"I take care of myself and end up in bed with the flu. Tom goes camping in the rain and doesn't even get a sore throat."

"Tanya has so many men interested in her, she has to turn down dates. I sit home alone. I'd even take her leftovers."

These feelings, in one form or another, are real for most of us at some time in our lives. And as the possibility becomes a reality, the devil, the father of lies, whispers in our ears: "You really got the short end of that deal. People ignored you. God doesn't love you very much. If he did, he wouldn't let this happen. You just can't trust him anymore." And then, in anger and hurt, we give in to jealousy.

What a distressing and defeated state of affairs. This is not the stuff campfire testimonies are made of! But what do I do? How can I love God when life is so unfair? How can I get over the jealousy and anger that well up within me when I see this awful unfairness?

Begin with Your Brain

We will all start at different points as we try to answer these questions. But, one way or another, as we deal with these hurtful emotions, we need to use our minds, our hearts and our spirits to overcome sin and find healing within. My mind looks at what I am thinking. My heart looks at what I am feeling. And my spirit worships God, in all of his grace and his truth. Of these three tools, or sources of information, the mind is the one about which we can be most intentional. Martin Luther reportedly observed that he could not keep the birds from flying around his head, but he could keep them from nesting in his hair. We cannot make our hearts or our spirits produce happy emotions or joyful inspirations. But we can make some choices about what our thoughts will do. So the place to start is with our brains.

I need, first of all, to look inside myself with as much honesty as I can muster. What am I really angry about? Are there changes I need to make in myself that will help me feel better about this situation? Should I use this anger as motivation to seek out someone and rectify a bad relationship? Or am I angry about something I cannot change? Do I need to ask God to help me let go of my anger? God, what do you want me to do with this jealousy and frustrating anger?

Then we can use our brains to think about God, his character, his creation and his values. What I *think* will influence what happens in my heart. I cannot keep the jealous feelings from cropping up, but I can talk back to them. I can talk back with conviction, conviction that is inspired by the Holy Spirit and Scripture and informed by the meshing of the truth that is found in my feelings and in my thoughts.

Here is what I could say to my heart when it is angry and jealous, particularly about the inequities of life.

God Is in Charge

First of all, I could tell myself that our sovereign, loving God can do whatever he wants. And apparently he does not want to be "fair." Jesus made this clear in his parable of the worker in the vineyard (Mt 20:1-16). He said that the kingdom of heaven is like a landowner who hired men in the morning to work in his vineyard that day. He said he would pay them a denarius (an average day's wages). A few hours after that, he hired more men. Later, he took on a few more. Twice again, later and later, he hired more men for his team. When the end of the day came, and the men lined up for their pay, they based their expectations on the Law of Fairness. But, guess what. The landowner didn't live under that law. He paid all the workers for the full day.

Most of us would have no trouble understanding the anger of those men who were hired first. "Whattaya mean?" they grumbled. "We were out there in the heat working all day for you. We deserve more pay than these guys who came in for the last hour. That's not fair!" Then the landowner said, "Oh, but it is fair. I gave you what I promised you. It's my option to pay the other men whatever I want." Then he asked a penetrating question, "Are you envious because I am generous?" (Mt 20:15).

When I consider my own jealousy, that question makes me ashamed of myself. Am I jealous because God has been good to someone else? How can I be so selfish that I do not want someone else to experience God's goodness just because I look smaller in comparison? Lord, forgive me.

God's Heart—God's Will

The second thing I could tell my heart in its jealous moments is the age-old theological truth that the providence of God reflects not his heart but his will. God's heart is set to be lavish in love and goodness. He does not want bad things to happen to good people. His *heart* is set against evil. But his *will* is to let people choose, even if they choose against his love. For some reason God has chosen not to destroy evil, point for point, as history moves along. His timing is different from ours. Because his providence allows goodness and evil to exist side by side, there will be times when life truly is unfair, in fact unjust.

When something terribly unfair happens to us, I imagine God is sad along with us. In his heart he loves us and grieves with us. But his will is to let us live in a world where diseases and crimes and tornadoes impact everybody, including good people, including people of faith. And it is a world where men and women are free to choose between good and evil, between fairness and unfairness. Sometimes people choose the wrong thing. And sometimes the choices we make, and others make, hurt people. I know, as a parent, how sad it is to see something unfair happen to my children. But even as a human parent, I often choose not to step in and right the wrong. God, our heavenly Parent, may not interfere either. Sometimes I need to tell my jealous heart that even though something seems terribly unfair now, one day God's justice will reign (Ps 73:18-20).

One Sunday morning our pastor spoke about hope. He said that Augustine once observed that Hope has two daughters: Anger and Courage. I sat up and listened. Anger? Courage? He explained that Anger sees things the way they are—and Courage sees that things will not always be the way they are now. I need this kind of hope as I confront the unfairness of life.

Grace vs. Fairness

Another thing I could tell my heart is that God is a God of grace, not of fairness. His grace is generous, giving goodness and forgiveness and love where they are undeserved. Grace is the ultimate unfairness!

Grace is giving when nothing is given in return. That is not fair. More often than not, my jealousy is rooted in the fact that I am nowhere near as gracious as God. And yet there is nothing I need in my own life more than the grace of God. Without his grace, I wouldn't even have a relationship with him where I could tell him about my jealousy. If only I could be as gracious toward my friends as he is toward me! God, help me to move in that direction.

One of the things I do to help me be more gracious as I battle with jealousy may not sound very Christian at first. Sometimes I recognize my jealousy and talk to God about it, but I still live in the grip of anger and ungraciousness. Since my jealousy almost always involves another person, I am hesitant to talk about it. I don't want to "gossip." But sometimes it seems to be too much to handle alone. I have two very close friends whom I think of as my "gossip friends." If I am so angry and upset with my jealousy that I cannot get out from under it on my own, I call one of these friends and say, "I need to gossip." Then I share the struggle I am having. As I talk about my anger, my hurt and my wounded pride, more often than not I begin to see for myself the falseness of some of my assumptions, the self-centeredness of some of my desires and the cosmic foolishness underneath my jealousy. That helps me let go of it.

This is not really gossip. Scripture teaches that if someone offends us, we are to go to him or her first (Mt 18:15). But my jealousy rarely grows out of someone else's offense. It is my problem, not the other person's. As I talk with one of my "gossip friends," I almost always find that I come out of the conversation more able to love the one who is the object of my jealousy. A better word than gossip is probably *confession*. As I confess my sins, or as I confront the lies I am believing, my friend stands by my side and supports me. Then she prays for me. Usually the rope of jealousy is cut loose from its grip around my heart.

Reality Check

A fourth thing I could do with my jealous heart is to perform a reality check on my own life. Jealousy usually means that I am valuing myself either too much or not enough. If my jealousy grows out of thinking too highly of myself (Rom 12:3), then I probably think others do not appreciate me enough and other people are getting honors I deserve. If my jealousy grows out of thinking too little of myself, then I probably am not recognizing and appreciating the particular gifts God has given me. Compared to others, my gifts look plain. Either way, my view of myself leads me to believe that life is just not fair.

The Creator God never intended that all of his children should look alike, act alike or have the same gifts. He did intend that we should all reflect some aspect of the Spirit (1 Cor 12:7). But that reflection is as different in each of us as our faces in the mirror. We need to remember whose idea it was that we be so different. "There are varieties of gifts, but the same Spirit; and there are varieties of services, but the same Lord; and there are varieties of activities, but it is the same God who activates all of them in everyone" (1 Cor 12:4-6 NRSV). Both jealousy and anger at life's unfairness often grow out of our unwillingness to embrace the theological truths of those verses.

Author Elizabeth O'Connor writes that "envy is a symptom of lack of appreciation of our own uniqueness and self-worth. Each of us has something to give that no one else has." This echoes C. S. Lewis's observation that "each of the redeemed shall forever know and praise some one aspect of the divine beauty better than any other creature can. . . . Each has something to tell all the others—fresh and ever fresh news of the 'my God' who is 'our God.' " As I learn to give appropriate value to my own unique gifts, then I am less apt to be jealous of others' gifts.

In my better moments I believe that I am a custom-made creation. God intended that my life should manifest some aspect of his character. He gave me a few gifts that will reflect his love as I use them. I have a temperament and a personality suited to use the gifts he gave me.

But when I forget that he designed me, I may be tempted to worry that I am not like someone else. Or I may be tempted to think that I need to be everywhere and do everything because the world cannot get along without me! Either way, I run the risk of anger and jealousy.

"Play to an audience of one." That's the advice one friend of mine gives. In my mind I picture one player, on stage alone, living life for one person in the audience, the Lord himself. In his sovereign and mysterious way, God takes my performance in life's drama, combines it with those of all his other children, and puts it together as one great meaningful production. I don't need to be jealous of the other actors in this drama because God himself is directing it, as well as sitting in the audience, applauding each of us as we use the gifts he has given us.

The Sanctuary of God's Love

Finally, I could talk to my jealous heart and remind myself to withdraw from the rush of life. This is what the psalmist did when he was almost overwhelmed with jealousy. He said that, at first, he could hardly handle the unfairness. "When I tried to understand all this, it was oppressive to me," he admitted, "till I entered the sanctuary of God; then I understood" (Ps 73:16-17). When he withdrew from the immediate pressures of life and thought about what he knew about God, then applied it to the situation at hand, he was able to conclude: "Yet I am always with you; you hold me by my right hand. You guide me with your counsel, and afterward you will take me into glory. Whom have I in heaven but you? And earth has nothing I desire besides you" (vv. 23-25).

My anger begins to dissipate (and with it, my jealousy) when I remember that my relationship with the living God is the most important thing in my life. My job, my friends, my talents and my honors all change over the years. But my relationship with God is forever. When I focus on his love and care for me, I realize that I do not need to be angry about life's unfairness. He will keep every promise he has made, in his time. Someday I will understand. In the meantime, I just need to remember that he loves me, when life is fair and when it is not.

Scripture for Reflection or Discussion

1. "Have you any right to be angry?" (Jon 4:4).
    This is the question God asked the prophet Jonah when he got angry that God was "gracious and compassionate" to the people of Nineveh. Because God is "abounding in love," he did not send the "calamity" on Nineveh that Jonah had predicted (at God's command). Can you think of a time when you have been angry with God? What precipitated your anger? What did you do with it? Looking back, with the benefit of objective hindsight, did you have "any right" to be angry?

2. "He causes his sun to rise on the evil and the good, and sends rain on the righteous and the unrighteous" (Mt 5:45).
    Rewrite this observation in your own words. What is unfair about this? Why do you think God allows such unfairness? How does his unfairness affect your life?

3. "Lowborn men are but a breath, the highborn are but a lie; if weighed on a balance, they are nothing; together they are only a breath" (Ps 62:9).

Do you see yourself as "lowborn" or "highborn"? How do others see you? How does your view of yourself affect you when you are tempted to be jealous of others? Is this verse "good news"? Why or why not?

4. "When I tried to understand all this, it was oppressive to me till I entered the sanctuary of God" (Ps 73:16-17).

Where is your "sanctuary of God"? When do you enter it? Do you like being there? Why or why not? What things would you like to understand better the next time you enter the sanctuary of God?

7

Is It Okay
to Be Ambitious?

The house lights were down in the theater. It was too dark to see the petite costumed figure positioning herself on stage. The play opened with quiet but urgent dialogue. Suddenly the quiet was shattered by a piercing scream.

"AUGHHHHHH!!"

It was my daughter. She was acting the part of Betty, a young Puritan girl who claimed to have encountered a witch in the woods outside Salem, Massachusetts, in the early seventeenth century. My daughter's scream alerted the audience to the central theme of her high school's production of Arthur Miller's play *The Crucible*. Miller portrays the evil, the broken relationships, the terrible anxiety created by suspected witchcraft. As I watched the drama unfold, I wondered how anyone could even think of getting involved in witchcraft, real or imagined.

It is unsettling, to say the least, to realize that the Bible speaks of witchcraft and jealousy in the same breath. Surely jealousy is not as sinful as witchcraft! This disconcerting association picks up even more momentum when we look at a list of other words spoken in the same tone as jealousy: sexual immorality, debauchery, orgies (Rom 13:13); quarreling, outbursts of anger, factions, gossip, arrogance, disorder (2 Cor 12:20); hatred, rage, idolatry (Gal 5:20-21). Such company jealousy keeps!

The common denominator in these evils is not their effect. After all, the baby conceived in the passion of an orgy is not in the same category as the hurt feelings left in the wake of an outburst of anger. The common denominator is, rather, the motivation of the heart in each of these acts. The verb form of the noun *debauchery* is *debauch*. To debauch means to "lead away from virtue." All of these acts, or sins, are the results of hearts that have turned away from the Prince of Peace.

Motivations of the Heart

I would never think of setting up an altar in my home to worship a foreign god. In fact, when my husband and I were looking for a house to rent, we rejected one because it was full of "art" which looked too much like idols to my mind. But if the truth be told, I do have an altar in my *heart* where I occasionally worship idols. It is those idols which have led me to many of the sins Paul listed in his letters to the early churches. I have had outbursts of sinful anger. I have acted in hate. I have gossiped. I have been jealous. I have been debauched. I have let idols lead me away from my God.

What do these idols look like? They certainly do not have the same physical appearance as the idols which tempted the Israelites in Old Testament times. They do not have a consistent shape and form. But they are not entirely unlike those idols. And the temptations they present are just as strong. The idols worshiped by the Israelites' neighbors were a very strong temptation to them. For some reason, the Israelites really wanted to worship those foreign gods. The bent of their hearts toward idols may have been like our bent toward materialism, power, intellectualism, perfectionism or other images of success. We may not physically prostrate ourselves before these idols, but we do sometimes live our lives hoping that we will please certain people, make certain impressions or be honored for certain accomplishments. Sometimes these desires are so strong in us that they invade our lives in much the same way the gods of the pagans influenced their societies. And these are often the very things which prompt us to be jealous. So perhaps Paul was right that there is a link between jealousy, debauchery and idolatry.

At this point, I cannot resist taking a theological risk. There is a wonderful picture of jealousy and idolatry in Ezekiel. In one of his colorful and impressive visions, Ezekiel sees the "idol of jealousy" (Ezek 8:3-5). When I consulted my friend who is an Old Testament scholar, he informed me that there has been discussion over the years about this passage because the Hebrew is not entirely clear. He warned me not to use these verses as the cornerstone of a major doctrinal discussion! But the idea behind the words intrigues me.

Even though we do not know exactly what this particular idol was, the fact that Ezekiel saw something which could be called an "idol of jealousy" suggests to me that jealousy may actually be a camouflage for idolatry. Is it possible that I am jealous because I am worshiping something or someone other than God? I think it is not only possible, it is *likely* that this is one cause of jealousy.

The Idolatry of Ambition

This is a particularly helpful word picture when we look at the relationship between selfish ambition and jealousy. One of the frequent and persistent causes of jealousy is our feeling that someone else is getting the success, honor or reward that we feel we ourselves deserve.

Ambition, by definition, is the strong desire to achieve something. The common use of the word *ambitious* conveys some of the same meaning as the word *proud*. *Pride*, used to mean an unrealistic view of one's own importance, is conceit, and that is a sin we want to avoid. I have chosen to use the word *ambition* because, even more than *pride*, *ambition* is a word like *jealousy* which has a "good" meaning and a "bad" meaning. Once again, the double meaning has to do with motivation and is very relevant to our understanding of the relationship between jealousy and ambition.

Paul said it was his *ambition* to preach the gospel (Rom 15:20). He urged the Christians in Thessalonica to be *ambitious* to lead a quiet life, win the respect of outsiders, provide for themselves and so on (1 Thess 4:11). Ambition, like jealousy, can have a good effect when its purpose is to promote the values of God's kingdom. Selfish ambition, on the other hand, promotes my own achievements, my own wished-for image, my own real or imagined successes. James wrote, "For where you have envy and selfish ambition, there you find disorder and every evil practice" (Jas 3:16).

I see both kinds of ambition operating in my life. I am ambitious about teaching the Word of God. I am ambitious about seeing people take steps toward embracing kingdom values. I am ambitious to see myself growing spiritually. But that same ambition has a very dark side. When I see my friends flying around the country to speak at conferences, or when I realize that my neighbor received more helpful counsel from another Christian friend than from me, or when I hear about a milestone of spiritual growth in someone else's life—then, I am ashamed to say, selfish ambition sometimes grips my heart and my mind with its jealous feelings and thoughts.

Upon closer examination, that selfish ambition sometimes reveals some disturbing questions: Do I think God would love me more if I did all these things which are provoking jealousy in my spirit? Would he value me more if I spoke at more conferences? Would he love me more if I gave better counsel? Would he like me better if I were growing faster? If I am honest about these questions, I conclude that God's grace grows out of his character and his will, and not in response to my actions. But (and this is a big but!) it's *the world* that will probably affirm me more if I do all of those things—speak, counsel, grow—and my pride wants my world's accolades. My ambition, then, is not for God's grace but for the world's affirmation. The approval of others becomes an idol to me.

Is this always what the idol of selfish ambition looks like? Not at all. It can take infinite forms. It can appear with many faces. This just happens to be one face I have unmasked in my own life. Let's take a closer look at the connection between ambition and jealousy.

Consider, first, the stories of envy and ambition which Scripture gives us in its biographical sketches of God's people. The first instance of achievement-oriented jealousy took place just outside the garden gate at Eden. Cain was jealous of his brother's "successful" sacrifice (Gen 4:1-12). God accepted Abel's sacrifice but rejected Cain's offering. We don't know exactly why God did that. Cain may not have found out either; he was too busy killing his brother in a jealous rage.

Later in Genesis we read story after story of the jealousy and ambition of Jacob with his brother Esau. Jacob stole Esau's birthright by appealing to his appetite, and then he stole the blessing Esau should have received from their father by tricking Isaac into thinking he (Jacob) was Esau. Apparently this ongoing destructive rivalry was not new: we read in Genesis 25:22 that Jacob had been fighting Esau even in the womb!

King Saul and His Jealous Eye

The account of David's journey to the throne is loaded with roadblocks put in his way by Saul's jealousy and selfish ambition. But jealousy interfered with David's life even before he met Saul. David's brother, Eliab, spoke in jealous anger to David when he came to the camp to see if he could help. "Why have you come down here?" Eliab asked. "And with whom did you leave those few sheep in the desert? I know how conceited you are and how wicked your heart is; you came down only to watch the battle" (1 Sam 17:28). David faced jealousy and accusations of jealousy even within his own family. Then, after he killed the giant Goliath with his slingshot, he faced jealousy again, this time over his military victory.

Saul was pleased with David at first. Then he heard the women of the town singing songs about how great David was: "Saul has slain his thousands, and David his tens of thousands" (1 Sam 18:7).

Now, watch it happen. "Saul was very angry; this refrain galled him. 'They have credited David with tens of thousands,' he thought, 'but me with only thousands. What more can he get but the kingdom?' And from that time on Saul kept a jealous eye on David" (1 Sam 18:8). He also brought his own life to ruin.

Centuries later, Jesus encountered jealousy and ambition in his disciples. First, they argued about who was the greatest (Mk 9:33-35). Later, John and James asked him if they couldn't please have seats of honor in the coming kingdom of God (Mk 10:32-40).

And Jesus' death on the cross was, from a human standpoint, the terrible result of envy and selfish ambition.

But these stories are also hopeful. Not only is God not surprised by our jealousy and selfish ambition, he does not even cover them up to make his people "look good." One of the messages of these biblical accounts is that God knows his people get jealous. He may not like our jealousy, but our jealousy will not keep him from accomplishing his purposes. This gives me hope and confidence to confront jealousy rather than hide it and to ask God to cleanse me and to use me in spite of my struggles.

It Happens Today

If Scripture were still being written today, what accounts of ambitious jealousy would God notice in your own life, in your neighborhood, in your church? I've been asking my friends that question for a year or two. Here are some of their answers.

One friend said that she thought ambitious jealousy in her office expressed itself as the desire for power. Every promotion is seen as a power play. The higher the job, the greater the prestige and the power. And the greater the potential for jealousy.

Another friend told me he struggles with the opportunities other people get at work which he does not get. He said, "Jealousy is a form of selfish competitiveness."

A retired business executive told me that jealousy hits in the corporate world as "frame-of-reference thinking" where success can be determined only with reference to the success (or failure) of other people. This way of thinking, almost by definition, includes the jealousy of comparison. I can succeed only if someone else does poorly, or, in reverse, for someone else to accomplish something, I must accomplish less. No wonder the rot of jealousy invades the workplace!

Twentieth-century jealousy also invades the church. Jealousy may be wandering through the coffee hour after the worship service: "I would have been glad to be on the committee, but no one asked me." (Translated by Jealousy: People don't value my talents and gifts as much as they do other people's.) "Well, I am on the committee, but I just don't see how I'm going to handle one more meeting each week." (Translated by Pride: I am so important that I am in constant demand.)

Another twentieth-century form of selfish ambition may come from an unhealthy desire for perfection. Sometimes it is hard to tell whether my desire to do something well, even perfectly, is rooted in pride and ambition or in wanting to please the Lord. A psychologist friend observed that it is one thing to try to make something "perfect" if its beauty causes you to give glory to God. It's something else to be *driven* to perfection. The difference is what happens internally. Relating this to jealousy, I would add that if I am jealous of someone else's accomplishments, and if that jealousy makes me work harder and thereby please my Father who also enjoys a "job well done," that is good. But if my jealousy leads to a compulsiveness to prove myself or to dissatisfaction even when I have done my best, then the selfish ambition to "be perfect" may be lurking in the corners of my life—and that is *not* good.

Ambition and jealousy may grow out of childhood wounds. Another friend, Carol, talked about going bowling with her singles group. She was astounded when she realized how competitive and ambitious she was that night. She was actually jealous of her friends' strikes and spares at the bowling alley! She could hardly believe she would stoop so low! Then she remembered how often her mother had reminded her that she must be the best. As she bowled, she was whispering to herself, "Mom would be so disappointed. I'm really a loser."

Carol's ambition and subsequent jealousy grew out of painful experiences in her childhood. That's true for a lot of us as we look at our jealous feelings. So do we throw up our hands and call it quits because we cannot reshape those early, impressionable years? Not at all. In making the choice to be honest about our jealousy, we can also choose to be honest about our ambition.

Perhaps you are ambitious because Mom or Dad did not give you enough affirmation, or they demanded too much, or they favored your sibling who achieved more. You can and should be very sad about that. But you can also ask God to transform past experiences and to help you move toward the future (Phil 3:12-14). In short, because you are a beloved child of the heavenly King, you can start acting like an adult. You can put childish, jealous notions behind you and move on, confident of his affirming love.

Starting to Break Free

There are at least three specific things we can do to move in that direction. They all involve *where we set our affections* in life. They involve our goals in life. They require courage to be different from our society. If our struggles are deeply rooted in past wounds, then we will probably need the help of a friend or counselor to change the perspective behind our compulsive jealousy. But we can at least begin the journey on our own.

The first thing we can do is *sharpen our focus on what is really important in life.* Jeremiah records what the Lord says about this: "Let not the wise man boast of his wisdom or the strong man boast of his strength or the rich man boast of his riches, but let him who boasts boast about this: that he understands and knows me, that I am the LORD, who exercises kindness, justice and righteousness on earth, for in these I delight" (Jer 9:23-24). To know God, to love his kindness, justice and righteousness—this is what is really important in life. Infinitely more important than my own successes or accomplishments.

The second thing we can do is *sharpen our focus on ourselves.* Scripture is clear. "Do not think of yourself more highly than you ought, but rather think of yourself with sober judgment, in accordance with the measure of faith God has given you" (Rom 12:3). "Each one should test his own actions. Then he can take pride in himself, without comparing himself to somebody else" (Gal 6:4). If we are going to overcome our ambitious jealousy, we will need to take our eyes off others and take a good look at ourselves. Coming to grips with our own limitations and shortcomings may actually be a little like offering a sacrifice. What we lay on the altar is our expectation for personal success. There are some things I will never be, do, or have. Ever. In some situations it is very hard to accept that. But in my better moments, I agree with author Joe Bayly, who said, "When it comes right down to it, Lord, I choose to be Your failure before anyone else's success."[1]

And the third thing we can do to free ourselves from ambitious jealousy is *be honest about the role of other people in our lives.* How much influence does the opinion of others have on me? How much do I define success by what others think success looks like? How much do I care about what other people think of me?

Jesus was very clear about this focus when he answered those who criticized him. "I do not accept praise from men," he said, "but I know you. I know that you do not have the love of

God in your hearts. . . . How can you believe if you accept praise from one another, yet make no effort to obtain the praise that comes from the only God?" (Jn 5:41-42, 44). Jesus was not talking to ambitious pagan opportunists. He was talking to the religious people of his day. He says the same thing to us. How can we believe if we are so busy trying to show off?

Our own ambition, then, may be an idol for us. The impression we make, the opinion others have of us, the immediate rewards for our work may be foreign gods in our lives. These gods promise contentment, connectedness, happiness. But they don't deliver. In fact, they leave us empty and hungry for the peace and joy which only God can give. These gods, furthermore, are a burden to carry around. Speaking of the idols of the Israelites, Isaiah wrote, "The images that are carried about are burdensome, a burden for the weary" (Is 46:1). Our preoccupation with the impression we make, our insatiable desire for affirmation, our perceived need for reward—carrying around all of these idols makes us weary. And, even worse, they deprive us of the experience of God's love. "Those who cling to worthless idols forfeit the grace that could be theirs" (Jon 2:8).

May God deliver us from selfish ambition and jealous pride which say we need more than he is offering us in his love and grace.

Scripture for Reflection or Discussion

1. Jesus described some of the religious leaders of his day: "They loved praise from men more than praise from God" (Jn 12:43).

In what ways is human praise different from God's praise? In what ways is it similar? Which do you like better? Which motivates you more?

2. "Their idols are silver and gold, made by the hands of men. They have mouths, but cannot speak, eyes, but they cannot see; they have ears, but cannot hear, noses, but they cannot smell; they have hands,

but cannot feel, feet, but they cannot walk; nor can they utter a sound with their throats. Those who make them will be like them, and so will all who trust in them" (Ps 115:4-8).

Do you agree that ambition can be like idolatry? Why or why not? What things are idols, or temptations to idolatry, in your own life? How do these things hinder your capacity to really live life as God intended?

3. "I also saw under the sun this example of wisdom that greatly impressed me: There was once a small city with only a few people in it. And a powerful king came against it, surrounded it and built huge siegeworks against it. Now there lived in that city a man poor but wise, and he saved the city by his wisdom. But nobody remembered that poor man. So I said, 'Wisdom is better than strength.'. . . The quiet words of the wise are more to be heeded than the shouts of a ruler of fools" (Eccles 9:13-17).

If you could choose, which would you rather have—wisdom, power or fame? Why? Do you agree that "wisdom is better than strength"? Why or why not? What area of your own life feels as if it might be "under siege"? What do you think might be the wisdom of the Lord for you in responding to that area?

4. "You are a man and not a god, though you think you are as wise as a god" (Ezek 28:2).

What is the area in your life where you most want to have control, to be a god? How do you try to exercise that control? What is the result? What difference would it make if you made a conscious effort to hand over that control to God? What changes would you need to make?

8

Sometimes
I'm Afraid My Life
Is Not Working

*T*he trip to the hospital would have been uneventful except that it was *my* body they were taking to the emergency room. From the moment I woke up that Saturday morning, I knew something was terribly wrong with my back. My self-prescribed treatment was, of course, the easy one: Take two aspirin and go to bed.

As the day wore on, the pain increased. After consulting every medical friend I had, I decided that the only responsible course of action was to go to the emergency room and subject myself to the diagnosis and treatment of the doctor on call. Several hours later, I arrived home in a drug-induced, pain-controlled haze, clutching the four prescriptions which were supposed to help me through the next few days, as I faced life flat on my back.

During those days, as my back healed, I thought a lot about pain. Pain is a lonely experience. No one can feel your pain for you. Pain is all-consuming. I could hardly pray. That first day I couldn't read. Even the entertainment of TV did not deaden the pain emanating from my back. Pain, when you are in the middle of it, almost always seems to be the worst you've ever had. I thought about all these things as I looked at the ceiling of the bedroom.

But the strangest thought I had was that in my pain, I was jealous. It began with my sense of complete powerlessness. I am used to thinking, talking and acting my way out of unpleasant experiences. But I could find no thoughts, words or actions that would make me feel better that day. I thought about my good friend Sara, who is experiencing very painful depression. I found myself comparing my pain to her pain. I actually said to myself, "What I wouldn't give to trade pain with her!" Even as I thought the thought, I knew it was stupid. If I could have traded places with Sara, in my better moments, I would not have chosen to do so. Sara's depression has been weighing on her soul for months. I have struggled with depression myself, and I know how dark it can be. No, I would not want to trade places with her. But the pain in my back distorted my view of reality. I just wanted to get out—out of bed and out of pain.

An Escape Route

Jealousy may be an escape route we use to try to avoid the pain in our lives. By thinking about Sara and comparing her pain to mine, I gave myself permission to feel sorry for myself. With my distorted sense of reality, I could justify my self-pity by saying I had it worse than anyone else. Looking back on that time in bed, the foolishness of this kind of thinking seems very obvious. But we can be equally foolish when we give in to jealousy rather than admit our painful emotions, which are more subtle than physical pain and usually do not heal as quickly as my back healed. We may be jealous because our lives are full of painful experiences—pain today, pain we brought into today from yesterday, pain left over from childhood.

Pain and Fear

One of the most painful emotions we experience is fear. In fact, psychologists tell us that fear can be a pervasive feeling that runs through almost all of our other emotions.

Fear produces a sense of powerlessness and victimization. It can take many forms. Like physical pain, fear is a very lonely experience. And in the same way we would like to "take two aspirin and go to bed" for pain in our bodies, we want to quickly and effortlessly resolve the pain in our souls. Jealousy may be an attempt to avoid admitting and confronting fear and other emotional pain in our lives.

Jennifer James writes that "jealousy is simply and clearly the fear that you do not have value."[1] Fear of worthlessness is just one of our many fears, but it is a good example of how we can use jealousy to avoid the pain that fear might bring.

Rather than face the fear and pain of being unimportant and therefore not worth very much, we may turn to jealousy as a "quick fix." For many people, it's easier to be jealous and blame others than it is to risk letting this fear grip our hearts. But jealousy, like my painkillers, only masks the problem. If I don't take the time, courage and energy to find out what is causing physical pain and what I can do to correct the problem, then I risk worse pain later on—or, in the case of some "silent killers," I may even risk death if I ignore the symptoms.

I did not enjoy taking care of my back. It scared me. It meant that I had to give up days of carefully scheduled plans. It was inconvenient. But I chose to listen to the pain and take care of my body so that I would not be sent back to bed later, clutching my bottles of pills.

Listening to the Fears of My Heart

I do not enjoy listening to my fears and the pain of my heart. In all honesty, I'd rather get angry at God or someone else than admit that my fears may be rooted in reality. My heart may whisper to me: "You're not worth very much. Other people are doing better than you are. People like others more than they like you. You may have some talents, but yours look like macaroni and cheese next to the filet-mignon capabilities of your best friend. Compared to other people, you really are a nobody."

What if these whispered possibilities are true? What if I really am a nobody? I don't like that idea at all. My fears that these whisperings are true prime me to listen to the countering whispers of jealousy: "You're not getting what you deserve. If you had the position so-and-so has, you'd be doing better. People would like you more if you had all his talent. God gave you a bum deal. You have a right to be jealous." With our view of reality distorted by the pain of fear, we may find it easier to listen to those whispers of jealousy than to face the fears of our heart.

But I have found that the only way to be free of fear is to face it. Freedom comes (slowly) when I take the time and the courage to ask, "Why are you downcast, O my soul? Why so disturbed within me?" (Ps 42:5).

The Many Faces of Fear

Fear, like jealousy, is a very private experience. We all have different fears. But we all fear something or someone. Fear was the first result of sin (Gen 3:10). The fear Adam and Eve experienced has been passed down, in one form or another, to every generation of the human race. My fear may not look like your fear, but we both are afraid.

Some people are afraid of abandonment. (Are they more prone to jealousy about friendships?) Others are afraid of being wrong, of loss of control or of being ignored. (Are these people prone to jealousy of knowledge, power or recognition?) Still others may be afraid that no one likes them or that their lives make no difference to anyone. (Are they, then, jealous of the attention given to others?) Fear is infinitely multifaceted. The jealousy which grows out of fear is multifaceted as well.

As we look at our fear and the jealousy which grows out of it, we can learn a lesson from the example of Jesus himself. Jesus, who was filled with the Holy Spirit, was led by the Spirit to a desert, where he faced severe temptation. My fears and jealousies sometimes lead me to places that feel dry like a desert. Is God really with me in these barren moments? It is comforting to know that the Spirit does guide us, even when we are in such desolate places. In the desert, Jesus was tempted. The devil offered him first food, then authority, then power. In each case, Jesus answered with Scripture (Lk 4:1-13). The Word of God became his weapon in fighting the temptations of Satan. In my own life, I know of nothing as dependable, as available and as effective as the Word of the Lord in fighting temptation, including the temptations presented by fear and jealousy.

Let's look at three of the fears which may provoke us to jealousy and what God says about those fears in his Word.

1. *"People don't like me."*

Most of us have experienced queasiness at some point about whether or not our friends, acquaintances and coworkers really like us. We have a variety of ways of evaluating popularity. Some people measure their social value by the number of friends they have. Others think in terms of depth of friendship. Others think of the number of times friends compliment them and, heaven forbid, even envy them! I am an introvert by temperament, so I fear that people may not like me because I can't party all night and still be a good friend to someone the next day. Some of my extrovert friends tell me that they fear they may not have personal worth because they are not friends with the "right people." All of these fears can lead to jealousy of those who have what we fear we do not have.

What does God say to all this? He says, first of all, that each one of us is custom-made, designed by the Lord of Creation. David wrote a prayer to God: "You created my inmost being; you knit me together in my mother's womb. I praise you because I am fearfully and wonderfully made" (Ps 139:13-14). God is not surprised that I am an introvert. He is not surprised that I have a shy side to my temperament or that sometimes I am afraid of people. And he is not surprised that sometimes I am jealous of others' ability to quickly jump into close relationships. He knew about all those things when I was still in the womb.

The second thing God says to us about our fear that people don't like us is that no matter who else doesn't love us, the King of the Universe does love us!

This is not to say that friendships are unimportant. But they must always be evaluated in light of the main message of the Bible: God loves us. He told the nation of Israel that even though a mother could conceivably forget the child she has borne, he will not forget his children (Is 49:15). One day each one of us will stand before God, alone. It is his love which will count then, not our friendships or our popularity. He loves us when we are lonely. He loves us when we are jealous. He loves us when we sin. He loves us when we succeed. We may not actually feel his arms around us—he has given us friends for that—but when there are no friends, his arms are around us still, "for the LORD comforts his people and will have compassion on his afflicted ones" (Is 49:13). This is a truth about God which we can apply to the fear at hand. I'm thankful for that.

2. *"I feel so helpless."*

Another fear that often haunts our lives is the fear that we can't handle things on our own. Helplessness haunts me when I realize that in many ways I cannot change who I am. I cannot change most of my circumstances. No wonder I envy my friends who don't have to deal with my set of weaknesses and disadvantages. And, if I am really honest, I may also admit I'm afraid that *God* cannot handle those weaknesses and disadvantages either! Sure, I've heard of occasional miracles, but I need to get through *today*. I'm not sure I can do that.

What does God's Spirit whisper to our spirits when we feel so helpless? God's Spirit spoke through the prophet Isaiah to describe his own meticulous power and infinite ability. There is nothing he cannot handle. There is no personal weakness or difficult circumstance that falls outside his love and power.

Do you not know?
  Have you not heard?
Has it not been told you from the beginning?
  Have you not understood since the earth was founded?
He sits enthroned above the circle of the earth,
  and its people are like grasshoppers.
He stretches out the heavens like a canopy,
  and spreads them out like a tent to live in.
He brings princes to naught
  and reduces the rulers of this world to nothing.
No sooner are they planted,
  no sooner are they sown,

no sooner do they take root in the ground,
than he blows on them and they wither,
   and a whirlwind sweeps them away like chaff.

"To whom will you compare me?
   Or who is my equal?" says the Holy One.
Lift your eyes and look to the heavens:
   Who created all these?
He who brings out the starry host one by one,
   and calls them each by name.
Because of his great power and mighty strength,
   not one of them is missing.

Why do you say, O Jacob,
   and complain, O Israel,
"My way is hidden from the LORD;
   my cause is disregarded by my God"?
Do you not know?
   Have you not heard?
The LORD is the everlasting God,
   the Creator of the ends of the earth.
He will not grow tired or weary,
   and his understanding no one can fathom.
He gives strength to the weary
   and increases the power of the weak.
Even youths grow tired and weary,
   and young men stumble and fall;
but those who hope in the LORD
   will renew their strength.
They will soar on wings like eagles;
   they will run and not grow weary,
   they will walk and not be faint. (Is 40:21-31)

Maybe I'm not so helpless after all. So far, I have made it through every "today" in my life. My helplessness, my power-lessness, even my jealousy—they haven't destroyed me yet. By faith, I believe that they never will. I believe that God is indeed a sovereign LORD who works for good "in all things" (Rom 8:28)—even in my apparently hopeless circumstances today. So I say to myself: "You go ahead and pout if you want to. Be jealous. Feel helpless. But I am going to believe God anyway. Self, you are wrong this time. God, I believe in you and you alone." Amen.

3. *"I'm just not important."*

Sometimes my jealousy and fears twist together into a particularly terrifying thought: Perhaps I am making no differ-ence at all in my world. Perhaps all those important people (whom I envy) really are as important as I think they are—and I am not important at all. It really would not matter if I had never been born.

This is indeed a terrifying thought. It is one which disturbed the author of Ecclesiastes. "As a man comes, so he departs, and what does he gain, since he toils for the wind? All his days he eats in darkness, with great frustration, affliction and anger" (Eccles 5:16-17). This author seemed to understand my feel-ings that sometimes things seem meaningless. It's a great comfort to me that God included these words in his holy Word. On days when my life feels meaningless and I am jealous of those who are so "important," I am comforted to know that God understands.

The spiritual "answer" to our sense of unimportance and meaninglessness is also hinted at in Ecclesiastes: "Then I realized that it is good and proper for a man to eat and drink, and to find satisfaction in his toilsome labor under the sun during the few days of life God has given him. . . . For it is now that God favors what you do" (Eccles 5:18; 9:7). The answer is really a nonanswer. "You cannot understand the work of God, the Maker of all things. Sow your seed in the morning, and at evening let not your hands be idle, for you do not know which will succeed" (Eccles 11:5-6). The "answer" is that we do not know now what will be ultimately important and what will not—what will be meaningful and what will be meaningless. We can only do what we sense we are called to do *now*. The results belong to the Maker of all things.

The "answer" is to have faith in him and obey him today. If others get more credit, seem more important, get more immediate rewards, that is God's problem, not mine.

Be Still . . .

"God is our refuge and strength. . . . The LORD Almighty is with us. . . . Be still, and know that I am God; I will be exalted among the nations, I will be exalted in the earth" (Ps 46:1, 7, 10). When I am weighed down by the unimportance and meaninglessness of my life, I need to be still and know that God is God.

In fact, *stillness* is one of the most effective tools we have as we struggle with our fears and our jealousies. When I take time to reflect on my life and meditate on scriptural truth, then his perfect love drives out my fears (1 Jn 4:18). In stillness, I remember that God is in charge. He gives life. He gives meaning. He gives love. He loves even me.

As I look at these fears, and at others in my life, I need to acknowledge an important truth: I may never be completely reassured about my fears. Fear almost always has to do with the unknown. And there will always be unknowns in my life. I can ask all the questions I want, and I can come up with as many answers as possible, but I will always end up with some things I cannot know for sure. There will always be some dreadful possibilities to fear. Elijah, the well-known Old Testament man of faith, was afraid Queen Jezebel would kill him along with the other prophets. His fear was so great that he wanted to die. "I have had enough, LORD," he said, "Take my life" (1 Kings 19:4). Sometimes my fears, too, have made me want to die. But I am encouraged by what happened to Elijah.

He saw a "great and powerful wind." But God was not in the wind. Then he saw an earthquake. But God was not in the earthquake. Then came a fire. But God was not in the fire either. (This says something about our propensity to be jealous of dramatic representations of God!) Where was God? God was in a "gentle whisper" (1 Kings 19:11-13). God never seems to shout at my fears. Instead, the voice I hear most clearly is his whisper. And sometimes that whisper is very faint indeed.

But even when I'm not sure I hear at all, God is there. The New Revised Standard Version translates the presence of God as a "sound of sheer silence" (1 Kings 19:12). To be perfectly honest, when I ask God about the fears and jealousies of my heart, the answer I sometimes receive is *sheer silence.* But God himself may be in that silence. And when I, too, am silent, I can often turn from my sinful heart to worship the God who is there and who knows and who loves.

My back was healed in a few days. My fears and my jealousies will take a lifetime. This side of heaven, I will struggle with my own set of fears, weaknesses, disadvantages and jealousies. But God knows all about them. And the promise of Scripture is that God is standing beside us, whispering to us, comforting us and strengthening us to be the people he wants us to be.

Scripture for Reflection or Discussion

1. "There is no fear in love. But perfect love drives out fear, because

fear has to do with punishment. The one who fears is not made perfect in love" (1 Jn 4:18).

Do you believe that "love drives out fear"? Why or why not? When have you (or when do you wish you had) experienced love driving out fear? What do you think it means to be made "perfect in love"?

2. "We were harassed at every turn—conflicts on the outside, fears within. But God, who comforts the downcast, comforted us" (2 Cor 7:5-6).

Make a chart with three columns. In the first column list several fears you have. In the second column note how each fear affects your relationships with others. In the third column note times when God has comforted you as you experienced each fear. Did he use other people, Scripture, circumstances or something else?

3. "Fear the LORD your God, serve him only" (Deut 6:13).

Define *fear* as it is used here. How do you account for the double meaning of the word *fear*? Do the different meanings overlap, or are they entirely different?

4. "Even though I walk through the valley of the shadow of death, I will fear no evil, for you are with me; your rod and your staff, they comfort me" (Ps 23:4).

Do these words describe you? Why or why not? If they do not describe you, what difference would it make in your relationships if you feared "no evil"? How would that influence you as you respond to people and situations that may provoke you to be jealous?

Why does a shepherd use a rod and a staff? How do God's rod and staff comfort us?

9

If God Loves Me, Why Can't I Have It All?

I love it when people ask my opinion. My good friends know that I am delighted when they ask me what I am thinking about, what big life problems I am solving at the moment! And I love it when people ask me if I am working on any writing projects. But it has been a strange experience trying to answer that question during the last few months.

"What are you writing about these days, Alice?"

"I'm writing a book on jealousy."

"Oh."

Oh. Just oh. A whole book on jealousy? Responses to my answer varied from silence to discomfort to astonishment. The idea of jealousy conjures up for many people an image similar to a rerun of Charlton Heston acting the part of Moses in *The Ten Commandments.* Heston/Moses stands on the mountaintop, stone tablets in hand, and shouts down, among other things, *"Thou shalt not covet!"*

I Want What You Have

The first thing many people think of when they hear that someone is jealous is that the person being described wants a possession or material thing that does not belong to him or her—probably it belongs to someone else nearby. That's coveting. And that's an embarrassing idea to most of us. We don't want to admit that kind of jealousy. It flies in the face of our assumed self-sufficiency as well as our real or pretended distaste for materialism. I certainly don't want you or anyone else to know that I wish I had what you have.

But whether we want to admit it or not, most of us are affected by materialism and covetousness. We cannot, then, complete our discussion of jealousy without taking a good look at our materialistic desires.

Moses may not have looked like Charlton Heston, and we don't know whether or not he actually shouted out the Ten Commandments, one by one, looking at the masses of people cowering below him, but we do know that the Ten Commandments are the Word of the Lord. To many, they seem like evidence that God wants to spoil our fun and cramp our style. The truth is that the Ten Commandments are a source of freedom from desires and compulsions that make us unhappy, unhealthy and unproductive when we give in to them.

First Things First

"You shall have no other gods before me" (Ex 20:3) is not God's way of saying, "I'm the best and don't you forget it." It is, rather, his way of keeping us from the agony of living our lives for gods who cannot help us live in joy and contentment. "Remember the Sabbath day by keeping it holy" (v. 8) is not God's way of making sure that Sundays will be long, boring days. It is, rather, his way of keeping us from having to work at maximum speed seven days a week. He made the world in six days. He rested the seventh day. What was he doing while he rested? I think he was looking around at his work and enjoying it because "it was very good" (Gen 1:31). When I obey the fourth commandment, I am freeing a part of my week to enjoy the fruits of my labor.

And when the Lord said, "You shall not covet your neighbor's house. You shall not covet your neighbor's wife, or his manservant or maidservant, his ox or donkey, or anything that belongs to your neighbor" (Ex 20:17), he wasn't saying "If you obey me, you can't have any of the things your neighbor has." He was, rather, freeing us from *having* to have our neighbor's things or relationships in order to be content.

In our materialistic Western culture, it is almost impossible to really believe that we do not need certain things in our lives in order to be productive and healthy. We may believe it Sunday morning when we hear the sermon, but it is more difficult to believe Monday night when we invite dozens of people into our living rooms in little electronic boxes. These beautiful people tell us that the tenth commandment is a lie and that we will indeed be happier, more influential or more lovable if we buy their cars, pantyhose or exercise equipment.

How does the Lord respond to the invasive, overwhelming materialism of our society? I hate to say it, but he lets us have it. He lets us have whatever our money can buy. I have never yet seen an angel of the Lord barring the entrance to the mall. Nor do I see God raining fire and brimstone down on our homes when they become too loaded with materialistic *stuff.* No, he lets us buy and buy and buy. And we get sick from it all.

When the Israelites were wandering around in the desert, they forgot all the things God had done for them. And they started to complain. "We want meat," they cried. "We're sick of this manna" (see Num 11). And so God gave them what they asked for, "but sent a wasting disease upon them" (Ps 106:15). That little verse is one of the most sobering ones in Scripture. What if God really does give me what I am asking for? And what if, as I receive what I want, my bones start to rot? Do I really want it after all?

I do not really understand why God lets us in the Western world have so much. But just as surely as the Israelites got sick from too much of what they wanted, we too get sick—emotionally, spiritually, even physically—from too much of too many good things. Covetousness, according to Haddon Robinson, president of Denver Seminary, is "craving more of what you have enough of already." Giving in to that craving makes us sick.

"Stuff": Blessing and Curse

Here in North America we have received what we asked for. We have almost every materialistic "blessing" available in the world. But according to those who have lived in Third World countries, we are in fact impoverished. I read one account of an American business couple who went to visit Mother Teresa as she ministered to the poorest of the poor in Calcutta. The two were so impressed with her work that they decided to stay on and work with her in India. But she sent them home, telling them that in all of the world, she had never seen the depth of poverty that she had seen in America—poverty of love and relationship.

Have we sacrificed relationships in our desire to consume? Have we looked to our possessions for the joy that only love brings? I have to remind myself almost daily that I will *not* be happier if I have this or that. I will still be *me*. And the me that I am will be at peace only when I am in communion with the God who loves me.

Most of us who live in twentieth-century North America would be horrified to be transplanted back two thousand years to the "primitive" time when Jesus lived. Talk about creature comforts and conveniences! Jesus' contemporaries hardly had an abundance of them. But Jesus seemed to think that they too needed to be warned about the dangers of materialism. "Watch out!" he said. "Be on your guard against all kinds of greed; a man's life does not consist in the abundance of his possessions" (Lk 12:15). He followed this warning with the parable of the man who built bigger and bigger barns to store all his goods, not realizing that he would die soon and not be able to enjoy any of the good things he had stored up for himself. "This is how it will be," Jesus said, "with anyone who stores up things for himself but is not rich toward God" (v. 21). I think about that story whenever I try to stuff one more thing into the small storage area under our basement steps. Am I building bigger and bigger barns, or am I appropriately enjoying all the good, beautiful things God has allowed me to have? Jesus' story (and the small storage area!) constrain me to challenge my own bent toward materialism—and to look to God to help me resist its destruction.

But letting go of our "stuff" and letting go of our jealousy of those who have more "stuff" is not a simple thing. We don't settle the issue once and for all. We must continually reevaluate and redecide.

I am reminded of the stories of those who fled China when the Communists took over. The accounts of that migration describe the roads leading out of China. They were strewn with "stuff" that the fleeing people took with them and then found they could not carry. Near the cities were things of minimal value—household goods and such. Farther away from the cities, the roadsides became cluttered with things of greater value—sterling silver bowls, expensive ornaments, valuable keepsakes. As the fleeing refugees got even further away from home, carrying their things mile after mile, the evidence by the roadside told of the choices they made. As they became more desperately tired and hungry, they could carry less and less. They let go of more and more precious possessions. Some died on those roads. Facing probable death, mothers took their babies, certainly their most precious load, wrapped them carefully and left them by the road, hoping someone would come along and care for them.

In similar ways, we all make choices about what we want to carry along the road of life. Do I want to burden myself with my possessions? Is it worth it to move into a larger home? Do I want to take the time to shop for just the right item? Shall I work overtime so I can earn enough money to buy that new furniture? Am I jealously trying to live a life of materialism and consumerism? The sad thing is that often we don't notice that we are making choices. We put things down on the roadside (our times of quiet and reflection, our values, sometimes our friends or our children) and we don't even notice they are gone, because we are so busy carrying the load we've kept. Sometimes it takes an unpleasant interruption to make us aware of our choices.

Interruptions like this may take the form of pain and struggle in our lives. These "trials" have a way of causing us to evaluate what is really most important to us. Jesus implied that if the man with the big barns had known he was going to die that night, he probably would not have spent his time reorganizing his grain.

How Much Value Do My Possessions Have?
Sometimes it takes great frustration and disappointment be-

fore I remember that my material possessions are not the most important things in my life. Pain and illness also have a way of making that reminder clear. When some kind of suffering pushes me against the wall, I ask myself, "In light of this experience, what really is important in my life? What do I want to hang on to, in the face of losing something else?" I never, ever decide that the answer lies in my possessions.

Their limited value was brought home to me when we moved across country from New Hampshire to Wisconsin. The representative of the moving company told us what insurance to get in the unlikely event that the moving van burned up with all our household goods inside. It was a gruesome thought for me! But when everything was loaded on the van and we were driving our station wagon across the interstate, I thought about my husband beside me and my two daughters in the back, along with my favorite houseplants and garden perennials. I knew that even if the moving van never made it, I had what was most important to me right there.

One danger of materialism, then, is that it makes false promises and prevents us from valuing what is most important. But there is another danger which may be even worse. Sometimes our possessions *do* make us happy!

My daughter played a beginner piece on the piano that described this perverse state of affairs:

Money can't buy everything!
Money can't make you a king.
Money may not bring success;
Money can't buy happiness!
But of one thing I am sure:
Money doesn't make you poor.
Money doesn't make you sad;
Money can't be all that bad!

There are days, quite frankly, when I love all my "stuff." Most of the time, I think this is healthy. God gave us the created world to enjoy. The problem comes when I move from enjoying my possessions to letting possessions rule my life—even *enjoying* their rule!

Possessions rule my life when my happiness depends on what I own. Possessions rule my life when they consume so much of my time and energy that I forget the Creator himself. Possessions rule my life when my focus is on building bigger barns rather than building better relationships. And they rule when my attempts to love a friend are overshadowed by my fierce longing to own what that person owns.

Jealousy may be a warning sign that we have crossed over from enjoying to worshiping what God has allowed us to have. When we think someone else who owns a certain camera or has the money for a certain vacation is happier than we are, then we should stop to hear what our jealous hearts are saying to us. When we continually and jealously protect our time so that we can tend to our "estate," then we should ask ourselves if we are worshiping a false god.

If our daydreams frequently focus on things to buy rather than on people to love, or when our cure for blues or boredom is a quick shopping trip, then we need to check our priorities. When jealousy, in the form of covetousness, interferes with our relationships, then we need to take a second look at our attitudes toward the *things* in our lives.

The Bible's View of Possessions

How can we guard our hearts from the covetousness and materialism that generate jealousy—jealousy which in turn hurts our relationships? Some days I think the answer to that question is that I should sell everything I own and go live on a desert island. But I have an idea that that would not really work. I would do better to focus my attention on the hints Scripture gives to help us live with our material possessions, in obedience and in the grace of God's love. Here are a few of the things Scripture teaches:

"Whoever loves money never has money enough; whoever loves wealth is never satisfied with his income" (Eccles 5:10). Scripture teaches that I will never, ever be fulfilled by what I own.

"When I fed them, they were satisfied; when they were satisfied, they became proud; then they forgot me" (Hos 13:6). Scripture teaches me not to be proud about what God has given me. And Scripture warns me not to wallow in false satisfaction and forget who gave me life and every good gift.

"People who want to get rich fall into temptation and a trap and into many foolish and harmful desires that plunge men into ruin and destruction. For the love of money is a root of all kinds of evil" (1 Tim 6:9-10). Scripture warns against an inordinate desire to get rich. It is not money itself which is evil, but the love of money.

"Keep falsehood and lies far from me; give me neither poverty nor riches, but give me only my daily bread. Otherwise, I may have too much and disown you and say, 'Who is the LORD?' " (Prov 30:8-9). Scripture says that our goal should be enough, not too much.

Verses like these are an effective weapon against covetous jealousy. I need to hide these verses right where jealousy hits—in my heart. "I have hidden your word in my heart that I might not sin against you" (Ps 119:11). I need to have them immediately available in my memory when covetousness washes over me.

There will always be people around me who have things that

I want. And television, magazine ads and store windows will continue to lure me. My heart, on its own, is not trustworthy. But the Word of God gives me reason to resist my heart's inclination toward materialism. The Word of God is the tool I can use to find peace in him who promised to give me all that I will ever need, including the desires of my heart.

Scripture for Reflection or Discussion

1. "Do not be overawed when a man grows rich" (Ps 49:16).
   We are all "awed" by different things. Think of a time recently when you have been "overawed" by a possession which belongs to someone else. What was it? What kinds of possessions are most likely to "overawe" you? What difference would it make for you to have those things? How do you manage without them?

2. "The one who received the seed that fell among the thorns is the man who hears the word, but the worries of this life and the deceitfulness of wealth choke it, making it unfruitful" (Mt 13:22).
   The verse is from Jesus' parable of the sower, where he describes what might happen to the Word of God as it is "planted" in various lives. To what extent do your possessions choke the Word of God in your life? Are there ways your possessions nurture his Word for you? If you were going to make one change to counter the negative effect of "the deceitfulness of wealth" in your life, what would it be?

3. "Better what the eye sees than the roving of the appetite" (Eccles 6:9).
   In what areas of your life is your "appetite" strongest? What do you long for that you do not have? How can you teach yourself the art of contentment, learning "the secret of being content in any and every situation, whether . . . living in plenty or in want" (Phil 4:12)?

10

Transforming Jealousy into Faith

*B*y *the time I was a senior at* the University of Maryland, I was actively involved in the campus ministry of InterVarsity Christian Fellowship. The mirror above the dresser in my dorm room was covered with notes to myself, reminding me to call students to invite them to Bible studies or just to encourage them in their faith. My schedule was peppered with meetings and appointments. My life revolved around the activities of the fellowship group. I wanted, more than anything else, to serve God during my last year on campus. But the truth was that I was so desperate to serve God that I knew little of his love and peace in my own life. I was discouraged and spiritually weary.

Usually I looked forward to returning to the dorm at lunch to check my mailbox. But during this season of discouragement, even my mailbox disappointed me. On one day in particular, I looked in the little glass window and saw the hoped-for mail. As I leafed through the day's arrivals, I found the monthly newsletter from InterVarsity's national office. It was a PR brochure, designed to let "the public" know what was happening in InterVarsity chapters across the country. The lead article in the issue in my mailbox that day was especially discouraging to me.

The article told about a young woman who was active in her InterVarsity chapter at a large Eastern university. She was on the leadership team. She was leading Bible studies. Fellow students were becoming Christians. She sounded like a wonderful person. In my own discouragement, I was jealous of her. *She must be a real dynamo,* I thought to myself. *I wish I could be like her.*

Somewhat against my will, I read on. I turned the page to finish the article. It gave more and more details about this girl's activities. Suddenly the light dawned. "Wait a minute!" I couldn't believe it. "No, it couldn't be."

As I read on, it became more and more obvious. The girl in the article was me! I read it again. Sure enough. The details fit. But it couldn't be me. God couldn't use me as he was using the girl in the article.

I called my staff member. "Harold," I said, "did you send in that report to the I-V newsletter last month?"

"Yep."

"Was it about me?"

"Yep." It *was* about me. Unbelievable.

That was, in fact, my problem. It was unbelievable to me that God could or would use me. I knew he worked through individuals, and I knew the promises of his Word, but I did not believe those truths applied to my own life. I knew my life from the inside out. I knew that my heart was "deceitful above all things" (Jer 17:9). I knew that my motives were not always pure.

I knew the rot. And I thought God could not really use me until I cleaned up my act. So I was jealous of others whom he was using. And that jealousy, which grew out of lack of faith, destroyed the joy I might have experienced at that time.

The Work of Belief

It is a sad commentary on life that sometimes we can be so busy serving God (as I was), so busy looking inward (as we do when we are discouraged, angry or afraid), so busy striving for recognition (as we do when we are ambitious), and so busy looking for security (from possessions and positions) that we do not do the real "work of God." We become so busy with ourselves and our own work that we do not do *his* work. God defines his work in a very different way from the way we talk about responsibilities, jobs and activities. "The work of God," Jesus said, "is this: to believe in the one he has sent" (Jn 6:29).

It is an amazing statement of grace that God uses us, even when we are not doing the "work of belief." He is not dependent on our work, our faith or our talents. But the older I get, the more convinced I am that the healthiest, happiest, most productive way to live is to do the work of belief first and let the results rest in God's hands. When I choose to believe in Jesus, the one God sent, then my confidence is in him and not in myself. Belief in him is one of the first steps in conquering my self-centered, self-conscious jealousy and other such sins. Then I'll be in better shape to relate to the non-Christian at the bus stop or to complete whatever "work" assignment the Lord wants to give me.

Doing the work of belief is not easy. When we are doing the work of belief, we will not always be happy. In fact, we may not even be neutral. Our feelings will often be intense. Ask any single person who passionately longs to be married. Is it easy to believe that God loves you more than any life partner ever will? Is it easy to wait for a godly spouse when the field is so full of people who have compromised their faith? Is it easy not to be jealous when others get married? No, the work of belief is rarely easy. It is hard to do.

When Jesus told the disciples that the work of God was to believe, they were skeptical. Perhaps it seemed too vague, too undefined for them. They wanted to know more. (Thank goodness for the disciples and their questions!) "What miraculous sign then will you give," they asked, "that we may see it and believe you? What will you do? Our forefathers ate the manna in the desert; as it is written: 'He gave them bread from heaven to eat' " (Jn 6:30-31).

Missing the Point

The disciples sound like me. They knew the Bible. They could even quote Scripture. But they ignored some of the facts and they missed the main point. The fact was that even though the Israelites ate manna, they were hardly a paradigm of belief. Their journey in the desert describes more about what happens when we *fail* to believe than when we do believe. If manna was the sign given to facilitate belief, it didn't work.

Jesus, fortunately, knew that. He said to the disciples, "I tell you the truth, it is not Moses who has given you the bread from heaven, but it is my Father who gives you the true bread from heaven. For the bread of God is he who comes down from heaven and gives life to the world" (Jn 6:32-33). Jesus was saying that he himself is the sign, the manna. The "sign" the disciples wanted is found in relationship with him. It is not tangible. It is not visible. But it is real.

Recently I had to leave my wedding and engagement rings with the jeweler for two weeks. During that time, I had no visible sign that I am married to Bob. Someone meeting me for the first time would not have been able to *see* that I was married. But I was just as much married during those two weeks as I have been during the last twenty-two years. The "sign" did not make me married. Our commitment and relationship to each other is what makes us married.

What "sign" could Jesus give us in order for us to believe? His life, death and resurrection certainly provide strong evidence that our belief in him is well-founded. But beyond the testimony of Scripture, there is probably no outward, visible sign that would permanently convince us to believe when we are in the midst of difficulties and doubts. If bread falling from heaven, water gushing from rocks and rivers drying up did not convince the Israelites, why do I think similar signs might convince me? Instead, "Faith is being sure of what we hope for and certain of what we do not see" (Heb 11:1). After Jesus' resurrection, Thomas wanted a "sign" before he believed. Jesus allowed him to see the sign, but he also said, "Because you have seen me, you have believed; blessed are those who have not seen and yet have believed" (Jn 20:29). Peter wrote to the early church, "Though you have not seen him, you love him; and even though you do not see him now, you believe in him and are filled with an inexpressible and glorious joy" (1 Pet 1:8).

God is not being unkind or unreasonable about his lack of visibility. The evidence in Scripture and the testimony of our hearts in relationship to him are more lasting "signs" than any other manifestation could be. Sometimes my heart doubts, and sometimes I don't understand Scripture, but God seems to say that I still have enough reason to believe. If he chooses to manifest himself in more obvious ways, as he does sometimes, then that is his choice. In the meantime, my "work" is to believe, even though I do not "see."

Believing without seeing is not only a spiritual phenomenon. Great literature is great because it goes beyond what the author "saw" as he wrote. Composers write beautiful music not knowing if what they "hear" in their minds will be what the audience hears in the concert hall. Scientists act "in faith" that something is true even though they cannot see it or prove it. In spiritual matters, the eyes of our souls may "see" what cannot be seen or felt empirically.

This work of belief takes on specific significance in light of my struggle with sin, and with jealousy in particular. My jealousies become irrelevant if my faith is based not on specific signs but on my own personal relationship with him. Jealousy compares, complains and frets. Faith says, "I believe God is at work in his own quiet, powerful ways, whether I can see it now or not." Jealousy looks at what it can see *now*. Faith lives in relationship to the *I AM* (Ex 3:14), who sees the present with the same sight as he sees the past and the future. Jealousy is not work. It is something we allow to happen to us. Faith is the work of believing. It does not just happen. It is the result of years of relationship with God, choosing to be dependent on his grace and choosing to be nourished by the disciplines of godly living.

What Is Faith, Anyhow?

What does belief look like—the kind of belief that overcomes even powerful temptations? Faith is, primarily, *choosing to remember.* "Remember the wonders he has done, his miracles, and the judgments he pronounced, O descendants of Israel his servant, O sons of Jacob, his chosen ones" (1 Chron 16:12-13). "Remember this, fix it in mind . . . I am God, and there is no other; I am God, and there is none like me" (Is 46:8-9). Faith is *remembering what we have already decided we believe.* And it is *living according to the truths that we are remembering.*

The opposite of faith is forgetting. God spoke through the prophet Hosea: "When I fed them, they were satisfied; when they were satisfied, they became proud; then they forgot me" (Hos 13:6). How could we forget the God who has helped us in the past? How could we forget the God who loves us—the God to whom we have wedded our souls? When we are in the grip of sin, we do forget. When we are torn apart by the unfairness of life, the inequities of reality and the piercing pain of jealousy, we forget who God is. Scripture is full of warnings against forgetting God. The evidence is that it is not only possible, it is quite likely that when we are tempted, we will forget our God.

Six Things to Remember

Faith, then, is making *a conscious effort to remember God.* It is instructing our hearts and our minds so that in the throes of our battles with sin, we will be able to remember. In our better moments, it is reminding ourselves what we know about God. I can think of six things we can remember about God. When we remember these things, our faith is strengthened.

1. *Faith believes that God is involved.*

The prophet Zephaniah warned his contemporaries: "At that time I will search Jerusalem with lamps and punish those who are complacent, who are like wine left on its dregs, who think, 'The Lord will do nothing, either good or bad' " (Zeph 1:12). Faith says that God will do something, even if we do not know what it will be. Lack of faith is a false complacency that says, "I am in control. God doesn't care, so I'll handle this myself." Unbelief does not bother to think about God and apply our knowledge of God to the situation at hand. Unbelief is lazy. The work of faith is to live as though God is actively involved in our lives, convicting us, helping us, loving us.

2. *Faith is crying out to God.*

Hosea described those without faith: "They do not cry out to me from their hearts but wail upon their beds" (Hos 7:14). Lack of faith wails in loneliness. Lack of faith is self-pity. It moans and groans, feeling that no one cares. Faith cries out to the God who hears. When Jesus cried, "My God, my God, why have you forsaken me?" (Mt 27:46), he was expressing not disbelief but faith. He was crying out in the anguish of faith when God seemed silent and distant. Faith cries out to the God who is there, even though he may not be seen.

3. *Godly faith is believing in the right Person.*

Someone said that "fear is faith in the wrong person." I would add that jealousy grows out of faith which is rooted in the wrong object. Paul wrote to the Christians at Rome that the ungodly "exchanged the glory of the immortal God for images made to look like mortal man and birds and animals and reptiles" (Rom 1:23). When we are jealous, we are putting our faith in some person, object or goal other than God himself.

4. *Faith looks for God.*

Scripture is clear that God's intent is to reveal himself and his will to us. "What may be known about God is plain to them, because God has made it plain to them. For since the creation of the world God's invisible qualities—his eternal power and divine nature—have been clearly seen" (Rom 1:19-20). Faith looks for the manifestation of God's invisible qualities.

God can reveal himself whenever and however he chooses. But his revelation is usually not in circumstances as often as in people, regular people. His revelation is in *me*—in my being, in my soul, in my personality, in my body. "God has chosen to make known among the Gentiles the glorious riches of this mystery, which is *Christ in you*" (Col 1:27). If I live to be a hundred years old, I think I still will be astounded by that.

Jesus in me. Jesus in you. Astounding. The revelation of God is as unique and personal as every human being. It may take a lifetime to overcome the fears, jealousies and sins which hide the Jesus within us from others, but, nevertheless, *Jesus lives in us* (Gal 2:20). Sometimes God reveals himself to us through his presence in others' lives, and sometimes his Spirit within us whispers directly to our spirits.

5. *Faith looks for God in ordinary events.*

Elizabeth Barrett Browning wrote a wonderful little poem:

Earth's crammed with heaven,

And every common bush afire with God;

And only he who sees takes off his shoes,

The rest sit around and pluck blackberries.

People of faith do not wait for spectacular miracles. They look for the extraordinary work of God in the most ordinary events and ordinary people. And as they see the hand of God at work, daily, in the most humble, subtle ways, they "take off their shoes" and worship.

Our pastor reminded us one Sunday morning that the miracle which happened when Jesus calmed the stormy sea (Lk 8:22-25) was not that Jesus could control the weather. Yes, that was spectacular. But, much more amazing: God was in the boat! The God of the galaxies, sitting in a regular, dirty fishing boat with ordinary people.

Faith looks for God in the boat. Our emotional boats may rise and fall on waves of praise and criticism. Or they may flounder on shoals of jealousy. Sometimes they seem to leak, almost sink, as we struggle with sin. But we need to remember that if God is in our boat, we are safe, whatever difficulties, failures or struggles we face.

6. *Faith is still. Faith is quiet. Faith is not in a hurry. Faith whispers.*

Elijah found out that God was not in the wind, not in the earthquake, not in the fire. God's voice spoke in a "gentle whisper" (1 Kings 19:11-13). Jealousy, in contrast, does not whisper. Jealousy shouts. Jealousy strangles. Jealousy is always in a hurry to see the final results. In our struggle with jealousy we may lose some battles because we take on the personality of jealousy. We begin to rush. We crush the gentle spirits within us. We live noisy, busy lives. We go too fast through life. As we hurry, hurry, hurry, we cannot hear God's gentle, quiet voice. We become so preoccupied with our own work that we fail to do the work of God, which is to believe. We get so busy that we fail to hear the voice behind us saying, "This is the way; walk in it" (Is 30:21).

But faith listens to that still voice and follows its direction.

One of the great joys of my life is discovering that faith like this works. I do not always remember to believe. But when I do remember, and when I do the work of believing, then that faith changes my life. I am no longer the girl who was jealous when she read the InterVarsity newsletter. I am also not the girl described in the article. I am, rather, a person in whom God has chosen to dwell. I do not need to strive to serve God. I do not need to be jealous of those who seem to serve him better than I do. Jesus lives in me. He accomplishes his purposes through me. My work is to believe in him. He is in my boat. That makes all the difference.

Scripture for Reflection or Discussion

1. "Now faith is being sure of what we hope for and certain of what we do not see. . . . By faith we understand that the universe was formed at God's command, so that what is seen was not made out of what was visible" (Heb 11:1, 3).

What visible things in your life help you have faith? What are some of the things you believe even though evidence for them is invisible?

2. "I pray also that the eyes of your heart may be enlightened in order that you may know the hope to which he has called you, the riches of his glorious inheritance in the saints, and his incomparably great power for us who believe" (Eph 1:18-19).

Think for a moment about the eyes of your heart. What do they see around you and within you? What would it mean for the eyes of your heart to be "enlightened"? What is your hope for yourself in this season of your life?

3. Jesus told Peter that his problem was that he did "not have in mind the things of God, but the things of men" (Mk 8:33).

In what areas of your life are you most apt to look at life through human eyes rather than the eyes of God?

4. "For since in the wisdom of God the world through its wisdom did not know him, God was pleased through the foolishness of what was preached to save those who believe. Jews demand miraculous signs and Greeks look for wisdom, but we preach Christ crucified. . . . The foolishness of God is wiser than man's wisdom" (1 Cor 1:21-23, 25).

What characterizes "the wisdom of the world"? What characterizes the "foolishness of God"? What is the relation between "miraculous signs," "wisdom" and "Christ crucified"? How willing are you to believe (and to be known as a believer) if your belief is considered foolish by your friends?

11

Finding Freedom Through Repentance

If belief is the work of God, then is unbelief sin? If you asked me that question, I would be inclined to say no. If you asked the apostle Peter, he would probably say yes. I would answer no because it is very difficult for me to think that unbelief is sin. I'm more apt to say, "But I can't help it if I don't believe!" After all, I tell myself, I have to be honest. And some of God's promises really are hard to believe.

But I think if we asked Peter, "Is unbelief sin?" he would say yes, unbelief is sin. Peter knew from his own experience what it feels like to be convicted of the sin of unbelief. From the start of his friendship with Jesus, Peter struggled with unbelief. One of the first encounters he had with Jesus was in his own fishing boat. He had been out with his men all night and hadn't caught a single fish. Then Jesus came along in the morning and told

Peter, "Put out into deep water, and let down the nets for a catch" (Lk 5:4). When Peter reluctantly did what Jesus told him to do, they caught so many fish that their nets started to break.

What would you have done at that point if you had been Peter? I probably would have been excited and impressed. I would have loved all those fish. They represented money, success, power. What a catch! This Jesus was quite a guy!

But Peter had a very different reaction. He fell down before Jesus and cried out, "Go away from me, Lord; I am a sinful man!" (v. 8). Why did he feel so sinful? I think it was because he was astonished at what Jesus had done. He hadn't really believed Jesus could do it. His unbelief, his lack of understanding and appreciation of Jesus' authority and power, made him feel so sinful that he did not think he should be in the presence of Jesus.

But it took more than a catch of fish to turn Peter around from unbelief to belief. I sometimes think that just one miracle would last me a lifetime. But our unbelief is not so easily conquered. After Peter had been with Jesus for months, he still struggled with unbelief. In fact, one of the more memorable of Peter's struggles came right after he made his famous "confession."

Jesus said to Peter, "Who do you say I am?" (Mt 16:15). Peter gave the right answer: "You are the Christ, the Son of the Living God" (v. 16).

But when Jesus began to talk about his suffering and death, Peter actually rebuked him. "Never, Lord!" he said. "This shall never happen to you!" (v. 22). Imagine telling the Son of the living God that he was wrong! But Peter did not believe that what Jesus said would really happen. Or perhaps Peter was saying that he *wished* Jesus were wrong, because he did not want Jesus to leave him. Whatever Peter's motivation, Jesus responded to Peter's unbelieving rebuke with strong words: "Get behind me, Satan! You are a stumbling block to me; you do not have in mind the things of God, but the things of men" (v. 23). Peter's strong emotional response to Jesus reflected human, not godly, thinking.

That is the essence of unbelief: believing in the values, conclusions and expectations of ourselves and the men and women around us rather than believing in what God himself says. I struggle with this kind of unbelief daily. I suspect it will be a lifetime struggle. Unbelief is behind my fears. Unbelief is behind my pride. Unbelief is behind my jealousy. And, I have to admit it, unbelief is sin.

Even though I have made my "confession" with Peter—I believe that Jesus is the Christ, the Son of the living God—I still struggle as I try to translate that belief into the realities of my daily circumstances and needs. It is difficult in light of my fears and ambitions, and it is difficult in light of my jealousies. Does this mean that my fears, ambitions and jealousies are sin? There are many good reasons for saying so, but it may be more helpful to think of fears, ambitions and jealousies as *temptations to disbelieve.*

Deep Truths—for Somebody Else

When I am afraid of something, I am tempted not to believe God's promises. I know what it says in the Bible—"Surely he will save you from the fowler's snare and from the deadly pestilence. He will cover you with his feathers, and under his wings you will find refuge; his faithfulness will be your shield and rampart. You will not fear the terror of night, nor the arrow that flies by day, nor the pestilence that stalks in the darkness, nor the plague that destroys at midday. A thousand may fall at your side, ten thousand at your right hand, but it will not come near you" (Ps 91:3-7). But when I am in the grip of fear, I may say to myself that these verses could not apply to *my* situation.

Or when I am full of pride and selfish ambition, I am tempted to disbelieve that God really meant what he said through the prophet Obadiah: "The pride of your heart has deceived you, you who live in the clefts of the rocks and make your home on the heights, you who say to yourself, 'Who can bring me down to the ground?' Though you soar like the eagle and make your nest among the stars, from there I will bring you down" (Obad 3-4). When I am feeling proud and ambitious, I think these verses must apply to someone else.

Or when I want to buy one more thing to wear or one more thing for the house, I am tempted to disbelieve Jesus' words of warning: "Do not store up for yourselves treasures on earth, where moth and rust destroy, and where thieves break in and steal. But store up for yourselves treasures in heaven, where moth and rust do not destroy, and where thieves do not break in and steal. For where your treasure is, there your heart will be also" (Mt 6:19-21).

Translated into relationships, all these temptations lead me to the temptation to be jealous.

When I am afraid, I am jealous of those who seem to have what I am afraid I need.

When I am angry that God seems unfair, I am jealous of those who seem to have received more of his goodness.

When I am proud, I am jealous of those who receive more honor, even though the honor may be from people and not from God.

And when I give in to jealousy, I am sinning by refusing to believe that Jesus loves me as fully and as completely as he loves any one of his sons and daughters. I am refusing to believe that he will meet every need I have, in his time and in his way. I am refusing to believe that when I do the work he has given me to do, I am doing a valuable service—whether or not it is as flashy, as applauded or as admired as someone else's work.

The temptation to jealousy is not sin, but sin is nearby. With Cain, I need to hear the word of the Lord: "If you do not do what is right, sin is crouching at your door; it desires to have you, but you must master it" (Gen 4:7). When I give in to jealousy, I open the door to the sin of unbelief.

Looking in the Right Direction

What do I do, then, when the sin leaps at me, wrestles me and sometimes masters me? Repentance is the only escape from sin. I can analyze, rationalize and otherwise try to explain my way out of my sin, but according to Scripture, Jesus' death on the cross is the only effective way to move from my sin into the presence of God. And repentance is the way we come to God, asking to be received by him because Jesus died for us.

When we repent, we confess to God that we have been looking in the wrong direction. We may have been looking at what others think. Or, limited by our own experiences, we may have been evaluating our lives according to our own standards and not God's. We have been looking at ourselves rather than at the Lord of love, grace and goodness. When we look at ourselves, we see ambitions, fears, material desires and jealousies. When we look at God, we see such overwhelming kindness that we repent of ever having looked elsewhere. "God's kindness leads you toward repentance" (Rom 2:4). How can I doubt his goodness when I take time to really look at his love and his sovereignty? When I repent of my unbelief, I tell God that I am so sorry I have grieved him by not believing his Word, his promises, his commands.

Jealousy says that God may not have enough love or power to care for me in the particular ways I think I need care. Reality tells me that sometimes Christians do experience tragedy. Christians die in wars. Christians die of cancer. Christians, like all human beings, live with unmet needs. In moments of unbelief, these realities make me wonder if my jealousy isn't right. But then I think of Christians I know and accounts I have read of people who have faced dangers way beyond my own experience and have found God there. Or I think about my own life and realize that I have not yet had to experience anything where the love of God was not with me.

This evidence of God's faithfulness does not mean that I don't care what happens to me, or that I can assume that my life will not be touched by evil. No, to believe means to act as though God is here and involved, to think about the truths I know from Scripture, and to worship God, in whatever way I can, in spite of my fears, my jealousies and my insecurities. This is where the "rubber hits the road" for many of us. This is when I need to believe in what I cannot see. In spite of all the confusing circumstances around me, I choose to believe that God is God, the *I AM*, who is here, now, with me. If I do not do this work of belief, then I need to repent.

Turning from Unbelief

What else can we say about repentance? Once again, it is helpful for me to put what I know in a list. (I have to-do lists, shopping lists—and now repentance lists!) I can think of five things that Scripture tells me about repentance which will help me when I struggle with the sin of unbelief.

1. *Repentance is simple.*

Sometimes it seems almost too simple. I want to confess my sin and then explain to God just why I sinned. I want to be sure that he understands how hard I tried. I want to be sure I include just the right words to trigger forgiveness.

But Jesus' promise to the criminal who was crucified beside him reminds me that my explanations and excuses are unnecessary. That thief on the cross did not have enough time, energy or knowledge to give a carefully worded confession. All he could do was to cry out, "Jesus!" He said very little: "Remember me when you come into your kingdom" (Lk 23:42). Not much of a confession in my mind. But Jesus answered from his forgiving heart. "Today you will be with me in paradise" (v. 43).

Sometimes when we are in the grip of sin, all we can do is cry out, "Jesus! Jesus, help me. I can't get out of this on my own. I am jealous. I am proud. I am sinning. Help! Please, help." And Jesus reaches out and forgives us. In fact, our helpless cry is just what he has been waiting for.

2. *Repentance brings freedom.*

"Where the Spirit of the Lord is, there is freedom" (2 Cor 3:17). The experience of repentance is surrounded by the freedom of the Spirit. His freedom sets the stage for repentance and is the result of repentance. Freedom allows me to come into the presence of God. And in his presence, there is more freedom. His freedom allows me to be honest about my failures, honest about my fears, honest about my need for his help in my life.

Without that freedom, I am trapped. I am trapped in the tension of wanting to obey God—and at the same time wanting some of the very things he does not want me to have. I am trapped by having to pretend I am someone I am not, by my passions and my desires, by the sin crouching at my door.

When I turn to God, when I repent, there is a release in my heart. Now I am free to acknowledge the tension I feel, the disparity between who I am, who others think I am, who I wish

I were and who God wants me to be. I am free to receive his love. I am free to be me, because I can live in the presence of the God who made me, who loves me, and who fills me with his Spirit.

In repentance, we are turning to face God. As we turn, we look away from the sin behind us; even more, we look toward our loving Father. Instead of judgment, we find acceptance. Instead of punishment, we find freedom.

3. *Repentance involves other people.*

When I repent, I tell God about my sin, but I can also be honest with my close friends. "Look," I can say, "I am more of a sinner than you know. I have (for instance) been green with jealousy. I am jealous of the stupidest things. I am embarrassed about my sin. But God has forgiven me."

Repentance was never intended to be a solo flight. James wrote, "Confess your sins to each other" (Jas 5:16). When I include others in my repentance, I am strengthening my faith and confirming my confession. I am asking others to pray for me and support me as I seek to be healed from my sinful nature.

Dietrich Bonhoeffer wrote: "It may be that Christians, not withstanding corporate worship, common prayer, and all their fellowship in service, may still be left to their loneliness. The final break-through to fellowship does not occur, because, though they have fellowship with one another as believers and as devout people, they do not have fellowship as the undevout, as sinners."[1]

When we repent and "confess our sins to each other," we move into a new dimension of fellowship. May God give us friends who can accept us as sinners rather than saints. May we be the kind of sinners who welcome other sinners into his place of grace. And may God give us courage to develop relationships where this can happen.

4. *Repentance allows us to experience God's love through other people.*

This is another reason, besides prayer and support, why we need to confess our sins to one another. It is often through other people that we discover that God still loves us, even though we have sinned. God became flesh so we would know his grace and truth (Jn 1:14). When Jesus lived on earth, he manifested God's love. Today, we manifest that same love for one another. Because Jesus lives in us, we have the capacity to love others in a way that reflects God's perfect love. This is almost incredible to me, but I have seen it happen.

I have seen people visibly freed from the emotional strain of sin as they confessed their struggles to me. I have been freed myself as I have repented of my sins in the presence of someone close to me. When others stand by, accept me and love me in spite of my sin, then I am more able to believe that God too loves me.

Sometimes freedom comes because our "confession" involves real sin. At other times freedom comes because we have talked with someone about what we fear is sin, whether it actually is or not.

As I looked over my coffee cup at my new friend Janet, I could see the tension and anxiety in her eyes. As we talked, she began to tell me all the things she thought were wrong with her. I did not try to whitewash the sin in her life, sin which she had committed and sin which had been committed against her. I did not try to "sober" her sin. My hope that day was simply that I could love her in the name of Jesus.

As the waitress refilled our coffee cups, the fear in Janet's face began to fade. I knew she had felt God's love when she stood up and gave me a big bear hug.

As Jesus prepared the disciples for his death, he told them

that they would continue his ministry. He prayed that God the Father would protect them when he was on earth no longer but they were here doing his work (Jn 17:11). One of our jobs in the world is to love other people and help them find the freedom of forgiveness.

When I confessed to my newly married friend the jealousy I had felt at her wedding, she didn't condemn me for my sin, nor did she tell me all the reasons why I should not have been jealous. I was grateful, too, that she did not take on the burden of my jealousy by feeling guilty that her wedding had been the breeding ground for my struggle. As we talked, she said things like, "Oh, that must have been hard!" and "Oh, I get it. You felt the way I used to feel when my single friends got married." Thank you, Jesus, for her love for me when I was jealous.

5. *Repentance is not the end of the matter.*

Repentance is not an admission that I have totally messed up my life forever. Rather, repentance on our part leads to redemption on God's part. God not only forgives us, he also redeems our sin. He takes what is evil and brings good from it. Joseph said to his brothers, who had sold him as a slave into Egypt, "You intended to harm me, but God intended it for good" (Gen 50:20). Hundreds of years later, Paul wrote a lengthy argument to the Christians at Rome, describing how God had brought redemption even out of human sin. Paul came to the conclusion that "in all things God works for the good of those who love him" (Rom 8:28).

George MacDonald writes: "I saw in it the richness of God not content with setting right what is wrong, but making from it a gain: He will not have His children the worse for the wrong they have done! We shall lose nothing by it: He is our father. For the hurting sand-grain, He gives His oyster a pearl."[2]

Can God make a pearl out of *anything?* Can God take even

my propensity to be jealous and bring something good out of it? According to his Word, God redeems. He may use my jealousy to motivate me to take advantage of opportunities to use my own gifts. He may use my loneliness as an opportunity to let me experience his presence. He may use my need as an occasion to help me see his creative provision. Believing that he will redeem is doing the work of the Lord. Repentance is the first step in doing that work.

Scripture for Reflection or Discussion

1. "If we confess our sins, he is faithful and just and will forgive us our sins and purify us from all unrighteousness" (1 Jn 1:9).
   Define *confess* and *sin.* In your own words, what four things does this verse tell us God will do for us when we confess our sins?

2. "You adulterous people, don't you know that friendship with the world is hatred toward God? Anyone who chooses to be a friend of the world becomes an enemy of God" (Jas 4:4).
   Why is *adulterous* an appropriate word to use when we sin and are unfaithful to God? In what ways do you flirt with the world? If God leads you, spend some time confessing your adultery.

3. "But he gives us more grace. . . . God . . . gives grace to the humble. . . . He will come near to you. . . . He will lift you up" (Jas 4:6, 8, 10).
   In what ways would you like to be more humble? How, specifically, would you like to experience more of God's grace in your life? When have you sensed that God is, indeed, "near you"?

4. "He who began a good work in you will carry it on to completion until the day of Christ Jesus" (Phil 1:6).
   List three good works which God has begun in your life. Now list three areas of sin where you see the beginnings of victory. (These could include your struggle with jealousy or any other struggle which comes to mind.)
   What do you see as the next possible steps in your life to stir up the good works and gain more victory over sin?

12

Letting God Release Us from the Jealousy Trap

*F**aith and repentance are part* of a larger, more encompassing experience which is perhaps the final antidote for jealousy: the experience of "letting go."

Even though it is not a theological or specifically biblical term, "letting go" describes for me the spiritual phenomenon of releasing our anxieties, giving up our compulsions to control, and relinquishing our desires for power in relationships—letting go of our pride, which causes us to want to be the Creator God instead of his created being. This reflects what Jesus said: "Whoever wants to save his life will lose it, but whoever loses his life for me will find it. What good will it be for a man if he gains the whole world, yet forfeits his soul? Or what can a man give in exchange for his soul?" (Mt 16:25-26). These words of Jesus come right after his teaching that "if anyone would come after me, he must deny himself and take up his cross and follow me" (v. 24). The more we are able to "let go" of our preoccupation with self, the more we are able to follow Jesus in the way of love.

Jealousy, in its self-centeredness, takes us in the other direction. As we honestly face our jealousy, try to untangle its threads, and confront it with faith and repentance, we are moving toward the experience of letting go.

An Invitation to Rest

Two word pictures in Scripture help me understand what letting go looks like. The first is in Psalm 131:

> My heart is not proud, O LORD,
>   my eyes are not haughty;
> I do not concern myself with great matters
>   or things too wonderful for me.
> But I have stilled and quieted my soul;
>   like a weaned child with its mother,
>   like a weaned child is my soul within me.
>
> O Israel, put your hope in the LORD
>   both now and forevermore.

Letting go is resting in the arms of God as a small child rests in its mother's arms. It is quieting my soul. It is having a realistic view of myself—a view that recognizes my dependency on God, who is both my father and my mother. In contrast, jealousy usually has too high a view of self: rather than recognizing dependency, jealousy thinks it has to fend for itself.

There is no more peaceful image than that of a baby who has just finished nursing at her mother's breast. The baby is content, satisfied, even satiated. As young Christians we too were satiated with the newness and freshness of our experience of God's love. The child in this psalm, now weaned, is also at peace. Like weaning, letting go is the experience not of a newborn baby but of an older child.

Milk is no longer instantly available to the child. In fact, milk alone would not satisfy him. Life is a little more complicated. He can no longer lie half-asleep in his mother's arms and drink his fill. But he is at peace. He may not know where his next meal is coming from, but he trusts his mother and rests in her arms. Letting go means that my soul within me is at peace, contented with all that God has given me, not anxious about what I do not have. My soul is safe within the circle of God's loving embrace.

That is the word picture of letting go that I would most often like to experience. When I have that kind of peace in my soul, I don't want to leave my Father's arms.

A Struggle That Ends

But there is another word picture of letting go in Scripture which is equally descriptive of my experience. It is found in the account of Jacob's life in Genesis. Jacob was one of the great patriarchs of the Old Testament. But he was also a man who knew what it was to be jealous and ambitious. His life had been full of temptation, intrigue and sin. En route home from a long exile, he stopped to rest for the night. Instead of resting, he spent the night wrestling with a strong, mysterious man (Gen 32:22-30).

I'm not sure I understand Jacob's experience entirely (we rarely fully understand another's spiritual experience). But I do know what it means to wrestle internally with temptation and spiritual oppression. I know what it is like to struggle because I do not really want to obey God. The only way to win is to lose.

And that's what happened to Jacob. By the end of the night, Jacob cried out for the man to bless him. "I will not let you go unless you bless me" (Gen 32:26). Sometimes this kind of thing happens to me when I pray. If I am praying about a very difficult temptation and I just can't seem to shake the anxiety associated with it, I cry out to God, "Lord, I can't do this! Please, bless me!" Perhaps Jacob's wrestling match had some of the same ingredients that my spiritual struggles have. Perhaps his experience was quite different. But in the end, I know that God did bless Jacob, and Jacob "let go."

Jacob's experience is encouraging to me because God not only blessed him, he even affirmed his wrestling match. After Jacob let go, the man (who apparently was God himself) said to him that he was going to change Jacob's name. His new name was to be *Israel,* which means "you have struggled with God and with men and have overcome" (Gen 32:28). Then God proceeded to give Jacob wonderful promises for the future (Gen 35:1-15). One promise was, "I am God Almighty; be fruitful and increase in number. A nation and a community of nations will come from you, and kings will come from your body. The land I gave to Abraham and Isaac I also give to you, and I will give this land to your descendants after you" (Gen 35:11). This is quite a blessing for the man who conned his brother out of his birthright and had to flee from his own home!

In fact, the name *Jacob* means "he grasps the heel." Jacob was jealously grasping for everything his older brother had, from the moment of birth. The figurative meaning of Jacob is "deceiver"—hardly a compliment to the man God was choosing to receive his blessing. It is encouraging that in changing his name, God not only did not condemn Jacob outright for all his sins, he actually affirmed him in his struggle. Because he would now go by the name "he who struggled with God," Jacob and everyone else would know that faith had not come easily to Jacob. And it was the man Israel, the one who struggled, that God blessed.

For Jacob, letting go was not an easy experience. Sometimes letting go of my jealousy, my anger, my fear, my unbelief feels like a huge struggle. I'm not sure I can do it. It reassures me that God blessed Jacob as he struggled—and that Jacob was successful in his struggle. And it reassures me that letting go and receiving God's blessing go together.

It Isn't Easy Letting Go

There are several reasons why letting go is so difficult. One of the reasons came into focus for me recently as I read the parable of the prodigal son.

According to Jesus' story (Lk 15:11-32), a certain father had two sons. One of the sons squandered his inheritance and returned home penniless. His older brother, on the other hand, had stayed home, helping Dad on the farm. When the younger son returned home, broken and repentant, his father received him warmly. This did not sit well with the older brother, who was angry and jealous. Jesus tells us that the kindly father said to his firstborn son, "My son . . . you are always with me, and everything I have is yours. But we had to celebrate and be glad, because this brother of yours was dead and is alive again; he was lost and is found" (vv. 31-32).

I have read this parable many times. Sometimes I identify with the younger brother and am very grateful for God's mercy. Sometimes I identify with the older brother and am rebuked for my resentment. On this particular day, I got stuck on the father's words "everything I have is yours." The Spirit seemed to say to me that day, "Alice, do you really believe that?"

"No, Lord, as a matter of fact, I don't. Everything can't belong to everybody. If you give something to one person, it can't belong to me too. If you love every Tom, Dick and Harry, you can't love me with that same love."

When I admitted my concern, it was as though my soul took a deep breath and said, "We need to talk about that."

Throughout that day, I talked to myself about my fear that God's love is limited. I mused on whether or not God could love everyone equally. I admitted to myself how much I am influenced by my experiences with finite human love. I know that my own love is finite. I can say that I have undying, endless love for my husband and my daughters, but, in fact, expression of my love is severely limited after nine at night, or when I am sick, or when I am overwhelmed with responsibility. I may say that these three most-important-people are always welcome in my life, but sometimes I just want them to *leave me alone.* Is God like that? Does he get tired of me? Are there too many people in his life?

As I mused, I came to the conclusion that God's love is not like my love. In fact, even though God chooses to compare his love to the love of mothers and fathers for their children, the truth is that his love for us is infinitely greater than any human love can be.

Scripture uses words that are beyond human experience to describe the love of God. "For as high as the heavens are above the earth, so great is his love for those who fear him; as far as the east is from the west, so far has he removed our transgressions from us" (Ps 103:11-12). Even as David penned words about God's love and acceptance of us, he acknowledged that it was too good to comprehend fully. "Such knowledge is too wonderful for me, too lofty for me to attain" (Ps 139:6). As high as high can be, as deep as deep can be, as far west as you can travel, as far east as you can go: that is the extent of God's love.

One of the reasons, then, that it is hard for me to let go is that *I do not always believe that God really loves me and that his love is abundant and never-ending.* Jesus used the father in the story of the prodigal son to help us understand our heavenly Father. But we dare not limit our appreciation of God's love to our experience of human love. When God says to me, "Everything I have is yours," he is not talking about finite quantities. Unlike human love, God's love is limitless. It is limitless in its mercy, in its availability, in its accessibility. When God loves someone else, he is not dipping into my bucket, taking out a little of his love for me and putting it into that other person's bucket. His love for others does not mean he has less for me. Such knowledge is indeed too wonderful for me. But when I catch a glimpse of it, my soul fills up with joy. I "let go" and I rest like a child in its mother's arms.

Another reason why it is hard to let go is that sometimes *my heart and mind are gripped with anxiety.* This happens to all of us at some time. I may worry that a coworker's promotion will cost me my job. Or a single person may legitimately wonder if the one she loves is going to marry someone else. Or I may be anxious that the church growth plan will fail because another idea was chosen instead of the one I thought would work best. When concerns like these assault us, jealousy is no longer theoretical or just unpleasant. The very thing that makes me jealous may have the potential to change my life.

It's these life-changing experiences that make me most anxious. I know what God's faithfulness looked like yesterday. I believe he will be faithful today. But what about tomorrow? Will he, can he, love me and care for me and bless me in the future? Can I really *let go* of my anxiety? Again, I find my answers and my reassurance in Scripture.

You Are Not Alone Out There

When Jehoshaphat was king of Judah and large armies from surrounding nations came to make war against him, he must have been anxious about the future, to say the least. He stood up in the courtyard of the temple and talked to God about his anxieties. The bottom line was "We're not strong enough to defeat this huge army!" I feel that way sometimes about my anxieties.

Jehoshaphat's actions after he prayed are a good example to me. He was surrounded by other believers who were able to help him when he was at the end of his own resources. Jahaziel was one of those believers, and when the Spirit prompted him, Jahaziel reassured Jehoshaphat: "Listen, King Jehoshaphat and all who live in Judah and Jerusalem! This is what the LORD says to you: 'Do not be afraid or discouraged because of this vast army. For the battle is not yours, but God's. Tomorrow march down against them. . . . You will not have to fight this battle. Take up your positions; stand firm and see the deliverance the LORD will give you' " (2 Chron 20:15-17).

Jehoshaphat listened to his friend. That's a good example for me. When we struggle with deep anxieties, we need a community of believing friends to help us. Sometimes I feel like the crippled man in Luke 5:17-21. I need other people to lower me through the roof to Jesus; I need people to pray for me. Sometimes I need people to listen to me and to tell me the truth, reminding me what Scripture says. Sometimes I even need close friends who can say to me, as Jahaziel said to Jehoshaphat, "This is the Word of the Lord." My jealousies and fears are very private experiences, but I dare not try to handle them entirely alone. Sometimes I cannot handle my life and my relationships by myself. I need others to help me.

A third reason that it is hard to let go is that *letting go just doesn't make sense.* If I don't promote myself, who will? If I don't get the raise, how can I pay the rent? If I don't flirt with men, I might not get married. And so it goes. Protecting my image, even if my actions are motivated by jealousy, often makes a lot more sense than letting go does. Asking God to take care of me, when I see no way he can possibly do that, seems like a foolish thing to do.

But another look at Jehoshaphat gives evidence again that faith is, indeed, being "certain of what we do not see" (Heb 11:1). Jehoshaphat won the battle without lifting a weapon. The enemy armies actually ambushed and killed each other. I'll bet that, when he was praying in the temple the day before, Jehoshaphat never thought *that* would happen! But he believed God against all odds. In fact, as they left for the battle, he reminded the people, "Listen to me, Judah and people of Jerusalem! Have faith in the LORD your God and you will be upheld; have faith in his prophets and you will be successful" (2 Chron 20:20). He even appointed people to start singing: "Give thanks to the LORD, for his love endures forever" (v. 21). Letting go means trusting in God's love and provision even when I don't understand how I will receive it.

There is tremendous relief in letting go. When I let go, I no longer need to protect "my image." I am free to be wrong. I don't need to worry about what others think. I don't need to figure out how to get ahead. If I let go of myself, I really have nothing more to lose.

When I let go, I am choosing to be "crucified with Christ," and "I no longer live, but Christ lives in me" (Gal 2:20). If I want to obey Jesus' commandments to love God with all my heart, soul, mind and strength, and my neighbor as myself, then the place to start is with his death.

It is only at the foot of the cross that we can begin to let go of jealousy and of every other sin that strangles our relation-ships. We come once, and then we come again and again, to let go of our anger, our selfish ambition, our fearful anxieties and our materialistic covetousness. Complete freedom will not come this side of heaven. But as we take up the cross daily, letting go of ourselves in the process—letting all our petty and possessive loves fade in the light of Jesus' love for us—we can begin to love others as God himself loves us.

Scripture for Reflection or Discussion

1. "Whoever finds his life will lose it, and whoever loses his life for my sake will find it" (Mt 10:39).

Write this verse in your own words. Think of one situation in your own life where you have found life by losing something else.

2. "I will . . . give him a white stone with a new name written on it, known only to him who receives it" (Rev 2:17).

In this prophetic verse, we are told that we will receive new names in heaven. If you were to give yourself a word-picture name which describes who you are today, what would that name be? What name would you *like* to have? What experiences in your life promote each of these names?

3. "Love the Lord your God with all your heart and with all your soul and with all your mind and with all your strength" (Mk 12:30).

Thinking about your own life, how do you define and differentiate between heart, soul, mind and strength? What does it mean to you to love God with all of these parts of your personality and life?

4. "Love your neighbor as yourself" (Mk 12:31).

Why is "letting go" a prerequisite for loving your neighbor? What conclusions have you come to for yourself as you have thought about jealousy, anger, fear, ambition and covetousness? What steps do you want to take to be more loving in your relationships to those close to you?

Notes

Chapter 1: Sometimes It's Hard to Love My Neighbor
[1]Henri Nouwen, *The Return of the Prodigal Son* (Garden City, N.Y.: Doubleday, 1992), pp. 42-43.

Chapter 2: There's Mildew In My Soul!
[1]*Webster's Encyclopedic Unabridged Dictionary of the English Language*.

Chapter 3: If God Can Be Jealous, Why Can't I?
[1]*Expositor's Dictionary of Biblical Words*, p. 358.
[2]*The New International Dictionary of New Testament Theology* (Grand Rapids, Mich.: Zondervan, 1978), 3:1166.
[3]Ibid.

Chapter 4: Why Am I Jealous When I Don't Want to Be?
[1]*Webster's Encyclopedic Unabridged Dictionary of the English Language*.

Chapter 7: Is It Okay to Be Ambitious?
[1]Joseph T. Bayly, *Psalms of My Life* (Wheaton, Ill.: Tyndale House, 1969), p. 48.

Chapter 8: Sometimes I'm Afraid My Life Is Not Working
[1]Jennifer James, *Success Is the Quality of Your Journey* (New York: Newmarket Press, 1983), p. 13.

Chapter 11: Finding Freedom Through Repentance
[1]Dietrich Bonhoeffer, *Life Together* (New York: Harper & Row, 1954), p. 110.
[2]George MacDonald, *The Flight of the Shadow* (San Francisco: Harper & Row, 1983), p. 31.